Taking the Biscuit

A Pawtobiography

TAKING THE BISCUIT

A Pawtobiography

(Or, how NOT to train your puppy!)

Puppy training advice with a difference, as featured in Dogs Monthly.

Fizzbomb Biscuit-Birkett

Matador
9 Priory Business Park,
Wistow Road, Kibworth Beauchamp,
Leicestershire. LE8 0RX
Tel: (+44) 116 279 2299
Fax: (+44) 116 279 2277
Email: books@troubador.co.uk
Web: www.troubador.co.uk/matador

ISBN 978-1783061-570

British Library Cataloguing in Publication Data.
A catalogue record for this book is available from the British Library.

Typeset in Aldine by Troubador Publishing Ltd, Leicester, UK
Printed and bound in the UK by TJ International, Padstow, Cornwall

Matador is an imprint of Troubador Publishing Ltd

This book is dedicated to Jimmy and John.

The Grandads I never met, but who would have been wrapped around my tiny paws just like everyone else.

And to Harvey and Korky.
My first canine and feline cousins who stuck around long enough to settle me in and are now chasing rabbits and mice in the sky.

Donations from sales go to aid animal rescue.

A note about the author

Fizz was born on a farm in peaceful and beautiful rural Yorkshire and moved to wild, dramatic and rugged coastal Northumberland to be with his devoted family.

He has never forgotten his roots and "herds" his many and varied toys around the garden, but it must be said, he barks with a distinctly Geordie accent.

Go right ahead punk, read my book

CONTENTS

BEFORE FIZZ

AFTER FIZZ

BEFORE FIZZ

CHAPTER 1

Why me?

"The only thing that should surprise us is that there are still some things that can surprise us"

My family are dog lovers and they sure as life love me unconditionally, even when I'm a bit naughty – or let's face it even when I'm **pure evil**.

Before I picked them, they did some doggie research but still felt that they couldn't find answers to all of their questions.

And it's fair to say, even though they had yearned for their very own dog to love for years and years, the reality was a lot harder than they had bargained for.

The rewards were also a lot more precious.

So I thought I'd write an account of our first year together to help others in the same position. You'll get our story, warts and all so you can learn from the good bits and the bad. This is not an official training book, just a trot through our ups and downs to help you through yours.

You know those irritating celebrities who have a baby then write a baby book or design their "own" fashion range without ever having done a drawing or seen a sewing needle in their

 1

lives, well this isn't one of those, none of us are experts – hell, we're still learning,

Our journey is broken into 2 parts; Before Fizz and After Fizz.

Before Fizz is pretty brief and describes the preparation they did before I arrived.

After Fizz, describes our life together through ups, downs and learning from mistakes. And boy, did we make some…

Enjoy!

Footie anyone?

CHAPTER 2

Clues for the clueless

"Patience is the companion of wisdom"

Ok, hands up all those who think having a puppy is an easy, wholly joyful, stress free experience?

- Those who said "yes" are mad and should never be allowed to own a dog - **ever**
- Those who said "no" read on…

Basic things you should know about puppies

We are fundamentally clever and will challenge you when you don't even realise it;

We are **not** born with a basic understanding of English; we will learn key words (mainly with the aid of treats) over time;

You will **never** understand barking, although we will make you understand what we want by adapting to your world – eventually – this again, **will** take time;

Poo is yummy; eating poo doesn't mean you are starving us to death. Although, there are times when you may be – read on;

Chewing humans, their clothes, furniture and treasured possessions is far preferable to chewing rope toys, balls or hide chews thank you very much;

We love to chase moving objects and expect to sink our teeth in when we catch them; balls, squeaky toys, small children, grandads…

We are **not** house proud and **will**:
- trail mud right through the house
- put wet nose marks on the patio doors
- roll in anything icky then roll around the carpet
- give ourselves a good shake **inside** the house after getting soaking wet **outside;** the splashes go a surprisingly long way…
- eat poo then lick your face
- put muddy paw prints on your beautifully decorated walls in order to sniff something completely invisible **to you**
- lick water from the toilet bowl (so be very careful with cleaning products and **always** keep the lid down guys)

Similarly, we are **not** garden proud and **will**:
- chew the heads off your flowers and plants, my special favourites are Japanese azaleas and flowering hebe bushes
- dig holes everywhere (well **I** loved the cat too, but they shouldn't have buried her in my garden…)
- make mysterious brown patches appear on your lawn
- drink from your water feature
- randomly leap into your water feature
- eat your solar garden lights
- chew the fence, garden furniture and garden ornaments. My Mum likes a quirky garden and had rabbits, moles and various other plastic creatures dotted around the place. I've made a few improvements and they no longer have ears, noses, hands or feet; much better.

No matter how much you spend on "proper" dog toys, we will still chase an old plastic plant pot around the garden for hours;

You **will** learn to pick up warm dog poo through a thin plastic bag – as a bonus, it's a sure fire cure for nail biting;

You will need **endless patience**, lots of love to give and decent (as opposed to boring) doggie treats (more about this later) for training.

Everyone becomes an expert, telling you how to train us – friends, neighbours, family. Hell – even people who have never lived with a dog in their whole life. Best advice is, ask the real experts – your vet, puppy trainer, experienced dog owners, but hey, don't be at all surprised if the "expert advice" is conflicting…

Kindness, consistency and reward are key. If you don't want us to do something (chase cars, bite, chew your favourite slippers, beg at the table for scraps) then stop us immediately. Don't laugh the first few times then expect us to change when it suits you. If you stop us barking when people come to the door, don't be surprised when we invite burglars in for a cuddle.

Reward us every time we get it right.

Decide on your rules **and stick to them** – are we allowed on the furniture, are we allowed upstairs, what can we chew, when do we eat? It's quite funny for a three kilo puppy to chew the clip in your hair. When that puppy becomes 15 kilos and rips your hair out whilst chewing the very same clip, don't start complaining. (Mum's hair has grown back now but she had to re-arrange her fringe at a jaunty little angle for a while.)

We have no morals; we will sniff your privates and follow you into the toilet – not necessarily in that order…

Puppies are hard work and need constant supervision. We need at least two decent walks, every single day, even Christmas day and scorching hangover days, in all weathers, even when there's horizontal sleet that feels like it's slicing into your face.

We don't come cheap; puppy pens/cages (or you can just let us chew your furniture when you have to pop out – your choice), warm and comfortable bedding, an old pillow is fine at first but soon becomes a bit shabby and too small, vaccinations, boosters, regular worm and flea treatments, microchips, pet insurance (which incidentally, seems to come with ridiculously high excess fees and ***Top Tip***: *read the small print, policies will often only cover you for a certain time or monetary limit.*)

We got four weeks free pet insurance with my chip poo bags, doggie toothbrushes and tooth paste (I kid you not!) puppy treats, collars, toys (a favourite toy may only last a week until it's chewed beyond recognition) leads, possibly doggy day care if you work all day and if you really care, puppy school. You may think you don't need some of this stuff, but you'll need most of it and why wouldn't you want the best for us? Then there's neutering, which of course is up to you but don't be thinking of having litters of puppies for profit because there are **huge** overheads like vet's bills, food, people deciding they can't cope and wanting their money back.

The list is endless and what are you going to do with any pups you can't find good homes for? Could you live with yourself if you let a cute and innocent puppy go to anyone you had a bad feeling about? I hope you said a big fat "No" there. Why not just leave that to the experts eh?

Most importantly of all, we need nutritionally correct puppy food, four times, every single day! **Still convinced you want a puppy?**

 6

CHAPTER 3

My parents are anoraks...

"Animals are much more content with mere existence than we are"

Let me set the scene:

My Mum and Dad are what are commonly known as a "professional couple" she has a Master's degree and works in Change Management. This gives her an uncontrollable urge to change stuff, for no apparent reason, **all the time!** He's a Health and Safety and Quality geek with a string of equally impressive qualifications and gets ridiculously agitated if he catches anyone, even perfect strangers, standing on a stool on one leg, especially if they have a chain saw in their hands.

In other words, ANORAKS.

After 23 years together, they decided they quite liked each other and thought maybe they should seal the deal and get married. Mum says you just can't rush these things, but for goodness sake, they'll need the crisps liquidised at their silver wedding party.

They've travelled the world, have seen the most amazing sights and met the most amazing people along the way but believe me when I say, they have **never** wanted kids. When I eventually arrived on the scene, one stupid person had the audacity to say "I suppose this is the child you've always wanted?"

"No" said Mum, delivering her very best withering look (she can freeze vodka at 100 paces, gets that from my Nana) "He's actually the **dog** we've always wanted!"

To prove my point, we once went to visit our neighbour's newly born twins. When they caught me licking the babies' faces, Mum said "Stop that Fizz, you don't know where they've been!"

They love to walk and have often felt a good long walk along the beach where we live is a wasted journey without a dog to share it with. Dad lodges with my Granny Midge in the countryside during the week to be near his work and there are some spectacular walks he just didn't do because it seemed a little pervy to walk on your own somehow.

The time never seemed right with work commitments and they didn't see any point in having a dog and keeping it locked in the house on its own all day. They watched a programme once where a family went out to work or school and left their dog in the house alone all day. The producers did the same to the Dad; locked him in a room with no TV, no books, and no music, just some water and a ball. He was demented within three hours…

Then a special set of circumstances happened – my Dad got a proper job where he didn't need to do 12 hour shift patterns and Granny Midge went part time. The hunt for the new addition to the family was on.

Me n' Tigger cozying up

 9

CHAPTER 4

Think we found our vet first...

"The cure for boredom is curiosity; there is no cure for curiosity"

The first idea was to rescue a dog from the local shelter. It seemed like the noble thing to do, so off they went. **Oh dear...**

Let me warn you, rescue shelters do fantastic work to rescue, revive and try to re-home pets and you should support them as much as you possibly can. **Always** consider adoption before opting for a brand new puppy and try fostering if you're not sure if you want a dog permanently, but these shelters are not for the faint hearted.

As they went round the shelter, looking at the dogs, the cacophony of barking was soon drowned out by my Mum's uncontrollable sobbing. She just couldn't bear that these dogs had been abandoned, some had been badly treated and they were now in what looked to her like dog prison. They'd soiled in their living space because there weren't enough volunteers to walk them and Mum wanted to take them all home.

Mum was a basket case; Dad was embarrassed...

Most of the dogs were either Staffies or Greyhounds. Both are beautiful breeds and would have been welcome in our house but with 2 little human boys running around Granny's house my Mum and Dad made the difficult and heart rending decision not to choose a dog that may have been damaged and maybe more easily freaked out than your average dog.

So, next stop was the internet and they Googled the keywords "puppies for sale". There are a huge number of sites advertising pups for sale but it's really hard to know where the reputable breeders are and how to avoid unscrupulous puppy farming. They fell for a gorgeous little liver and white, 10 week old, Dalmatian and sent an email to enquire, leaving contact details…nothing happened.

They checked a few more, left more contact details…again, nothing happened.

The internet seemed a pretty futile place to look for the perfect pet so, not really knowing where to turn, they popped in to the local vets to ask about breeds and breeders. There are a lot of vets where we live so they just chose the one on the High Street - St Francis Veterinary Care. They were bowled over by the friendly staff who talked to them about different dogs then sat them down with a massive book that described each breed and its common characteristics. Mum and Dad described their circumstances and the veterinary nurse suggested a Labrador, a Springer or a Border Collie and also suggested they try the small ads in the local pet shops.

Often, this vet would be presented with a poor, unfortunate dog with an unwanted pregnancy and they said they would keep a lookout, but couldn't guarantee the background of both parents.

Everyone they asked, told Mum and Dad that it was **vital** to at least meet the mother and preferable to meet the father so

11

that they can establish the nature that the puppy is likely to inherit. Never, **ever, ever,** buy a pup from a breeder who doesn't let you meet Mum. The people at St Francis's told Mum and Dad, regardless of which vet they chose, they were to bring their dog in for puppy cuddles.

My Mum and Dad spent an hour in the vets and decided, if these people were so interested in matching the right pet with the right family, they were the ones for us. In essence, they'd found the vet before they found the pet!

They left promising to bring the new pup in to meet them; whenever that might be…

There are some excellent vets in our area but we've later found out that some vets are not in the slightest bit interested in puppy cuddles or helping owners find the perfect pet. Our vet sends out monthly newsletters to advise you about common ailments and how to treat them, how to cope with bonfire night and scary fireworks, why chocolate is **very** bad for dogs, how to get a pet passport, the last one described the common problems encountered with anal sacks – yuk – but useful! They told us that dogs yawn when they're content – blimey, I'm one super content dog, I almost turn my face inside out! They even sent us a message on Facebook when they saw my pictures….cool!

Choose your vet very carefully, feel absolutely free to check them out and reject them if they don't give you 100% confidence your pet will be in the safest and most caring hands should they need them.

It's **vital** that vets are in this business to care for animals and not for the pure pleasure of making a profit.

 12

Our team lost again today, didn't they Dad?

Our vet also offers you 4 weeks free insurance without any obligation to commit to a policy. There's more about our saintly vet's practice later.

CHAPTER 5

Home cooked ham and chips

"Anything worth doing, is worth getting someone else to do"

Ok, so now they knew that when you buy a pup, it's important to at least meet the mother. Meet the father too if possible (I mean, we've all read Marley and Me, right?)

After the Internet experience, Mum went into work feeling a bit dejected and unsure where to turn next. A chance conversation with my Aunty Fee turned her world around! Aunty Fee's friend Barbara, who runs a farm, had two litters of fabulous Border Collies due in December. She was only expecting one litter from Meg and Jem but the little slut Poppy had slipped past her and Gentleman Jem forgot his manners, so two litters were due, two weeks apart.

If Mum played her cards right, Aunty Fee would put a word in. I mean, you don't get a purebred, International Sheepdog Association registered Collie out of the blue. Collies are quite possibly the cleverest dogs in the world but Mum and Dad weren't looking to spend wads of cash, they really just wanted a mutt!

Mum didn't get too excited. Why on earth would Barbara let one of her fabulous pups – decedents of supreme champion sheep dogs be a family pet, a pet it must be said, destined to be a beach bum?

But hey...Aunty Fee worked her magic and Barbara agreed that Mum and Dad could have a pup and brought Mum photos of Meg and Jem. Hurrah! Now they just had to wait for the pups to be born (Barbara estimated around the 7th December) and go pick the one they wanted – or so they thought!

No surprises that Barbara was exactly right and we were born on 7th December, the anniversary of the bombing of Pearl Harbour; more about that later. In my litter, there were four boys and two girls. Of the boys, there was one with a distinctive spot on his head, me with a spotty front leg and a spotty nose, another boy with a kind of pirate's eye patch going on and an extremely handsome boy with a plain white flash on his face.

The two girls were very pretty but Mum and Dad had already decided on a boy because the neutering process is less stressful and easier for boys and by default, also less stressful for their new "parents".

Mum and Dad couldn't wait to meet us but this was a harsh and cruel winter and they just couldn't get from Newcastle to Yorkshire until I was almost four weeks old.

Fortunately, Barbara sent regular photos to Aunty Fee, who in turn sent them to Mum and if I say so myself, we were a fine looking litter.

We lived in the house for a while, then in the barn with Meg and had a lovely cosy kennel to sleep in and a safe place to run around. Barbara lined our play area with newspaper so we could go to the toilet. Mum and Dad favoured "spotty head" on all the photos, however, there was a little boy who seemed

to be getting jiggy with a "Page 3 Girl" – he looked quite interesting.

Aunty Fee said our markings could change as we got older and to be fair, they weren't much bothered, so Mum and Dad decided to just wait and see us all before making a decision.

In mid-January, they made the two hour journey using the new Sat Nav toy Dad got from Santa…oh boy, big mistake! Barbara had given Mum directions to the rather remote farm where she lives. Geography isn't Mum's forte and she directed Dad the wrong way up, or was it down? the motorway. The Sat Nav woman started getting ratty telling them to turn around – they ignored her.

Eventually, they realised they were heading in the wrong direction – Sat Nav woman had been right all along, and they retraced their way back. About an hour late, they turned up and met the lovely Barbara and her husband Pete.

Before they set off from home, Mum rang to say they were on their way and Barbara had offered to make them ham sandwiches and chips on arrival. Not wanting to put her to any trouble, Mum said "Oh no! don't go to any trouble" and Dad went mental – I mean, fancy refusing ham and home-made chips from a farmer's wife! Dad secretly checked their marriage certificate, I mean, there could have been some mistake…

They brought Mum's cousin John for the ride and a third opinion! He slipped and fell in the barn and I've kept running around his legs ever since to make him do it again, it's a hoot.

As soon as they arrived, Barbara brought them into our barn.

We stayed out of sight in the kennel for a little while because we weren't used to anyone but Barbara and Pete and occasionally their grandchildren coming to see us. Barbara opened the kennel roof, lifted out my brother – Handsome Harry – and handed him to Mum. Oh boy, she was so impressed with him, he was so very nearly **the one**.

But then, I trotted up to my Dad and started licking him. He picked me up and put me in his coat so we could sniff each other properly. He handed me to Mum and I went to sleep on her lap and we all agreed in that moment, we were just meant to be together. We were all pretty impressed and I decided I would keep them.

Spotty Head trotted out to see what was going on – just a tad late, I'd already beaten him to them, then all my brothers came out for a look. Pete said Pirate Patch was the dominant male because his tail was always in the air and his ears were upright – blimey, I'm enough trouble for most folks so I bet he's a right handful.

Just to be sure, they went to see Poppy's pups too and even though they were little beauties, we were already a family. Mum felt a bit guilty about Spotty Head and fretted about him all the way home but she still loved me best.

It's fair to say, they didn't want to leave me, but I still needed Meg and because the winter had been so horrible, we were taking a bit longer to wean onto proper food. Barbara promised regular updates and said she would ring when we were ready to leave.

Barbara, Pete, Mum, Dad and Uncle John went into the house for a cup of tea. Barbara seemed to instinctively know that my Dad likes his tucker and gave them lovely cake. Not

 17

quite ham sandwiches and chips, but it stopped him tapping Mum's head shouting "hello" every five minutes.

They met Meg – a real bundle of energy and extremely beautiful, Jem, a magnificent yet gentle soul who loves being stroked and scratched and my granddad Scot, a big, strong, handsome boy. They met noisy Lynn and beautiful Lucy and a few of the other dogs who share the farm with Barbara and Pete.

Barbara had prepared my family tree going back **five** generations with absolutely no "inter-breeding" to make us nuts. Blimey, my Mum and Dad can't trace their folks back that far!

We are all International Sheep Dog Association registered and Barbara showed them pictures of some of her previous dogs. She's clearly besotted with her dogs and has Collie mugs, calendars and pictures all over the place.

Mum got a little nervous at that point and asked Barbara if she minded that here I was, a "platinum pooch" destined to run up and down our beach, as a much wanted family pet, very unlikely to even meet a sheep! But all Barbara wants for her beloved puppies are responsible owners and happy, loving homes – phew!

Barbara said that if at any time, they couldn't cope with me, they should just bring me straight back. Blimey, just how much bother could I be?

And if you haven't guessed by now, I was the one getting jiggy with the "Page 3 Girl."

Me and the Page 3 Girl...

CHAPTER 6

What's in a name?

"The things that come to those who wait are usually the things left by those who got there first"

It's pretty fair to say that my Mum has an addictive personality and threw herself wholeheartedly into preparing for my home-coming. She project managed the whole thing with endless lists, in minute detail and with military precision. Dad was demented.

Aunty Fee was going to lend them a puppy cage for home. They decided to buy another one for Granny's so they didn't have to lug them around all the time.

Now, I know a lot of people agonise over whether to cage or not to cage. But really there are a few simple rules:

- the cage should be the right size for the breed – if you don't have an Aunty Fee, pet shops and vets will help you. Too big and we won't feel secure, too small and we'll be incredibly uncomfortable;
- they should be a snuggly safe haven, with cardboard on the floor, topped with a lovely soft cushion or pillow and something safe to chew, something we can't choke on if you're not watching, a rubber ring, a ball (that we can't swallow), a rope toy, a hide chew;
- they should **never** be used as punishment;
- you should never leave us in there for hours on end, except at night when we're all asleep;

- you can stop using them when your puppy learns not to eat your expensive furniture and designer shoes when unsupervised.

If it's the words "cage" or "crate" that freak you out, think of them as a nesting area, a den or a puppy bedroom.

Whilst out shopping, Dad announced: "I'm going to buy our dog a pen"
Mum: "Don't be soft, he can't write"
Dad: "Not a pen, a pen"
Mum: "What, like a memory pen to keep his photos on?"
Dad: "No, a pen, a puppy pen thing"
Mum: "Oh, a puppy pen. God, that was a bit like the two Ronnies Fork Handles sketch"

And they both fell about laughing – they do that quite a lot. Mad as hammers.

In a short space of time, Mum had gathered:
- a huge pile of toys (3 of everything, 1 for home, 1 for Nana Tosh's house and 1 for Granny Midge's house)
- food bowls
- water bowls
- boxes of poo bags *(**Top Tip:** shop around, nappy bags are cheaper and you can get perfumed ones and sometimes food bags are even cheaper again, but be careful they're not so thin that your fingers go straight through them – come to think of it, swinging a see-through bag full of dog poo isn't especially tasteful. Mum offered our neighbour a bag of poo for his lunch as he cycled to work as a joke and he was sick!)*
- grooming brushes
- pillows for my cages, with matching pillowcases that have my name written in felt pen so they don't get mixed up

21

with Mum and Dad's in the wash!

- cages, sorry, puppy bedrooms,
- a name tag (*Top Tip: Aunty Fee said to put our surname and phone numbers on it – not my name as it would be easier for someone to try and steal me if they knew my name*)
- a big box of puppy food
- puppy treats (*Top Tip: be careful to read the labels, some puppy treats are not suitable until we're three months old and don't buy adult dog stuff at first, we have delicate little tummies*)
- a puppy training book, which Mum reads to me, in the hope I'll conform to type - sap!
- "Chew Stop" to stop me chewing stuff (never in a million, I actually like it!)
- Spray stuff to stop me peeing and pooing on the floor (ain't gonna happen)
- Puppy training pads to make me pee/poo where they wanted me to (suckers!)

Naming me was never going to be easy. Mum is a **huge** Oscar Wilde fan and wanted to call me Oscar. Dad, for no apparent reason, wanted to call me Skippy and said a quite categorical "No" to Oscar. Mum was never going to agree to Skippy and declared I should be Darcy, after Mr Darcy in Pride and Prejudice – the Colin Firth one, of course. Dad refused to shout "Darcy" up our beach for fear of being beaten up by local thugs. "Colin" was also ruled out on the basis we have a friend called Colin and didn't want to confuse anyone.

Everyone wanted to know my name, but Mum and Dad just couldn't agree.

At work one day, Aunty Fee said she'd had a glass of champagne over the weekend and it was really fizzy. She got to thinking that Fizz was a really cool dog name. Mum went loopy and asked if she could have that name for me. Lovely Aunty Fee said – "OK"

At home that weekend, Mum asked Dad what he thought of Fizz. **Whoop, Whoop**, he liked it. They agreed it was perfect because they wanted me to be bubbly and sparkly, although many's the time since, they wish they'd called me Snoozy or Patience!

Now let me tell you, my Mum is a deep thinker and the name Fizz had conjured up something far grander in her head. Getting Dad to agree to Fizz was the first step, then she said:

"You know he was born on the anniversary of the bombing of Pearl Harbour?"

Dad: "Yeeeeeeessssss"
Mum: "And you know when we went to France they miss-spelt your name, calling you Mr Biskett?"
Dad: " Yeeeeeeeeeessssss – where is this going?"
Mum: " Well I was thinking…"
Dad: "Oh, no – I hate it when you think, what now?"
Mum: " Well I was thinking, we should call him Fizz Bomb Biscuit Birkett"
Dad: "Sheepdogs have one or two syllable names like Jem, Meg, Peg, Bob, Ben, Penny, Poppy. No, No, absolutely not in a million. His name is Fizz. Just Fizz. Maybe Fizz Birkett. Nothing more. Fizz it is".

Needless to say, may name is Fizz Bomb Biscuit-Birkett.

My snuggly wuggly puppy den

24

CHAPTER 7

"I've had the school on the phone…"

"Light travels faster than sound. That is why some people appear bright until you hear them speak"

While Dad was in denial, Mum tried my name out on a few friends.

Aunty Fee and Aunty Jules loved it;

Aunty Sandra didn't;

Aunty Margaret, Aunty Joan, Aunty Annette, Aunty Janet, Aunty Maureen, Aunty Tina, Aunty Nicola and Aunty Anne just accepted it;

Uncle Neil thought it was weird but rather likes Fizzy;

Uncle Ray was relieved 'coz he thought they'd give me a stupid name…

Aunty Janis thought Fizz Biscuit Bomb Birkett was far better 'til Mum pointed out that Biscuit Birkett had a silent hyphen. Stupid woman.

Generally, Mum didn't much care. Her mind was made up and eventually, even Dad accepted the inevitable.

Now that the hard work to find a name was done, Mum, Dad

and the rest of the family have decided to re-arrange my name so that I now answer to:

- Fizz – obviously
- Fizzlet
- Fizzbitz
- Fizzle
- Fizzbomb
- Fizzy
- Fizzogg and erm,
- Spotty chops, baby, gorgeous boy, my angel, precious, snuggles and skootchie – SKOOTCHIE?

It's a good job I'm an intelligent dog, but I'm asking you nicely, **do not** put **your** puppy through this, decide on a name and stick with it. Use it often so they know that you want their attention. They'll probably still ignore you, but it's the principle…

And for goodness sake, don't give them a confusing name like Joe or Brad because they might not distinguish that from "No" and "Bad."

Next, Mum went on the internet to find puppy training classes in our area. She rang two or three, but frankly didn't like the sound of them much over the phone, let's face it, no-one was going to shout at Fizz Bomb Biscuit-Birkett… One of them even said "have a look on our website" like she couldn't even be bothered to discuss her business – Mum was not impressed.

But then, a girlie night out sorted all that when Aunty Linda recommended "Pawfect". She'd taken her "Holly" there and they'd all loved it.

So Mum got straight on the Internet and looked them up.

They seemed positively Pawfect.

A class was starting on 14th March. According to Mum's plan, that would be two weeks after my second injection. Pawfect. This class would teach basic obedience and maybe I would learn something too? Mum signed up.

Mum is a clever person in lots of ways, but technology trumps her every time. So when it got to paying, she couldn't get past the PayPal bit (dork) and sent an email saying she'd just send off a cheque.

A couple of days later, my Dad rang her at work and said "We don't even have a dog yet and I've had the school on the phone…"

It seems the application and the email had crossed in space. All was sorted fairly easily.

Puppy school was booked, they just needed a puppy!

CHAPTER 8

The Homecoming

"You always root for the underdog, unless the other dog is yours"

Barbara kept Mum up to date with our progress and agreed that I could leave Meg on 5th February. The weather was still foul but we were weaned enough at eight and half weeks to leave home.

Mum and Dad hooked Sat Nav woman up and set off once more for deepest, darkest Yorkshire. They put a couple of toys, poo bags, treats, an old towel and my pillow in the car.

It was a really awful night with freezing fog and then Sat Nav woman decided not to charge up and died just at the tricky bit of the journey. Maybe she was still sniffy about the fact they ignored her in this very spot a few short weeks ago?

Determined that they were coming to get me, they soldiered on, in horribly adverse weather conditions and arrived, once again, an hour late.

When they arrived, me and Barbara were having last minute puppy cuddles. She bravely and unselfishly handed me straight to my Mum and had a little treat in store…

There in the house, was my Grandmother, Dolly. A really beautiful, almost regal, tri-colour Collie. So Mum and Dad had met Meg and Jem, my natural parents and Scot and Dolly, my maternal grandparents. All massively impressive in every way… they had to pinch themselves!

Barbara had fed me at about 9am that morning but didn't give me any more food in case I was car sick. Let me tell you, I was bloody starving but didn't make any fuss.

Pete rubbed my towel on Meg and gave it to Mum and Dad so that I would have a familiar smell in my new home. Barbara gave them a **MASSIVE** bag of the puppy food that I was used to, with some already mushed up for me when I got home, some basic instructions on how to look after me, details of my flea and worming treatments and my family tree.

She then gave Mum a pound coin for luck. Mum said they were already lucky to have me. I was really going to test that theory but we've kept the pound in a very safe place – under a little Border Collie ornament in our kitchen. We call it the Lucky FizzQuid!! We rub our lottery tickets on it; we haven't won yet but we're hopeful.

We got in the car, I sat on the pillow on Dad's knee, which he covered with Meg's towel and off we went. Still an awful night, the fog was even worse than before and the journey took far too long.

It must be said, that whilst I didn't show any inclination to play with the toys they brought, I was an exemplary pup on the journey home. I nestled contentedly on my Dad's knee, slept most of the way, woke up a couple of times, sniffed the air, got Daddy kisses and nodded back off again.

I didn't pee, poo or be sick and my new Mum and Dad thought I was the most perfect puppy in the whole wide

29

world…bless. I would soon prove them wrong, but for now we all enjoyed the equilibrium.

First stop was Nana Tosh's house. She'd bought puppy treats and put them in my bowl at her house. It's true to say, I've never forgotten where to look for treats at Nana's and whilst I love her, I go straight to my bowl or my toy box every time I visit.

Nana Tosh is soooooo house proud that she told Mum not to bring a dog in her house - **ever**. "No filthy animals in here – no way, no how" Mum says Nana will die with a duster in her hand.

But, she took one look at me and melted, I have her wrapped around my tiny paws...I give her Fizzkisses and she's completely under my spell. I'd get away with murder at Nana's house and when I go to stay from time to time she always says I'm as good as gold. Clearly, she lies beautifully, as the scratches on my Grandad's head tell a very different story.

Nana thinks I'm a great kisser and she's teaching me to dance. I'm pretty good at ballroom, well even a fox can trot apparently, but I'm useless at the Latin numbers. Besides, Dad won't let me wear the frilly shirts and tight trousers so it's pretty pointless.

For some bizarre reason, Mum had washed the floor and tidied the kitchen for me coming home – can anyone explain that one? At home, I was fed delicious puppy mush, we went into the garden for a little stroll, came back in again and I literally peed and pood all over the kitchen. Ahhhhhhhh, I'd soon have this place in shape …

They put my Meg towel in my cage with my lovely soft pillow, my toys and some water and when it was time for bed, I just went quietly into the cage, let them lock me in and I went to sleepypoos. I stayed there quietly until the morning. No fuss at all.

Sadly, the night wasn't so peaceful for Mum and Dad. Mum didn't sleep a wink, listening out in case I cried. When she finally did drift off at around 3 in the morning, she woke up 5 minutes later with a start and shouted "What if he's hung himself on his rope toy?"

Dad checked the insurance policies the next morning to see if he would suffer any penalties for strangling her under extreme duress.

"SIT"

AFTER FIZZ

CHAPTER 9

Separation issues and helping Mum at work

"In theory there is no difference between theory and practice, in practice there is…."

So, here we are. Mum and Dad have lived in this house for over 20 years, it's immaculate, they've had it all to themselves all that time and suddenly, I burst on to the scene.

Cream leather sofas, slub weave silk cushions, draped voile and lace curtains, sparkling glass tables and not a speck of dust or a finger mark anywhere. I have so much to do to make this place like home.

I need to sniff everything. I was only allowed in the kitchen to start off with, that's ok, our kitchen is massive and we live in there anyway. They were especially worried when I went anywhere near cables because I like to chew stuff, but they let me sniff anything I want – under strict supervision.

They were particularly keen that I didn't go upstairs, actually going up is ok, coming down is **really** dangerous for us puppy types. Never, ever let puppies use stairs. At first, they even had to lift me off the decking onto the grass in the garden. But pretty soon I could be found balancing on top of plant pots and exploring the rockery.

At five months old, I could manage the stairs easily, but still come rampaging down them like Eddie the Eagle, scaring them witless. I usually stand across the stairs stopping them going up and bite their ankles when they try to come back down. Once, I tripped Mum as she was coming downstairs and she crashed into a plastic tub of emulsion paint she'd left there. It went everywhere – especially when I had a little splash about in it! She doesn't leave paint at the bottom of the stairs any more.

Mum and Dad took a week off work to settle me in at home. They really wish they'd taken more time. But anyway…

After the first week, the plan was, on Monday mornings, me and Dad would set off early for Granny Midge's house, we'd have breakfast and he'd go off to work, leaving me to have a little snoozy in my cage.

Granny Midge would get up and we'd have a little stroll around the garden. She goes off to work at about noon.

Dad would come home at 1pm-ish and we'd have some grub and another stroll in the garden. We'd play with my ball for a while then I'd have some "quiet time" in my cage when he went back to work.

Dad and Granny Midge get back about 5ish and it's back in the garden, teatime and then we all play 'til bedtime.

On Fridays, me and Dad would jump in the car and go home to Mum and spend blissful weekends together.

That was all fine in theory, I could even hear the soft music in the background, but Mum and Nana Tosh suffered severe "separation issues" and couldn't bear to be away from me for that long.

As planned, at the end of our first week, Mum and Dad took me to Granny Midge's house and set up my new **huge** cage. They had followed the instructions on the internet and bought a cage with a picture of a Border Collie next to it. I tell you what, all three of us could have moved in comfortably and there it was - too big for Granny Midge's country cottage kitchen – in her newly decorated living room, with brand new cream leather furniture. This cage was roughly twice the size of my cage at home, but I still wandered in and made myself comfortable.

The following evening, Sunday, Mum had to leave me and wouldn't see me again until Friday.

Whilst I slept, blissfully unaware that she had even left, she was sobbing her lungs out driving along the A69. Dad fretted until she rang to say she was safely in the house. When she rang, I was happily playing in the garden with Dad, she told him to put me on the phone and he pointed it at me whilst she shouted my name and blew me kisses. I just thought…mmmmm, what's that he's giving me? He must want me to chew it.

So I did.

He deliberately lied when he told Mum I was wagging my tail when I heard her voice, but the ritual continued for months.

Also, Granny Midge had a 14 year old cat, Korky, who hated me on sight. The arrangements had to be reviewed, and pronto.

So the reality is, Mum gets up with me and Dad at daft o'clock

34

on Mondays and takes me walkies or in the garden 'til he has a shower and shave. She blubs when we leave, but then rearranged her diary so she could work in Newcastle on Fridays.

This means she does a 104 mile trip to pick me up on Thursdays and works from home on Fridays.

If she needs to do tele-conferences from home, she takes me to Nana Tosh or Grandad for intensive spoiling sessions and comes to get me as soon as she can.

She tried to do tele-conferences with me at home but I like to bark at the drain pipes, birds and my favourite plant pot. Besides, every now and again, I'd find one of my squeaky toys and rampage around the kitchen with it. I also like a bit of attention and need to chew and bite her when I don't think I'm getting the right amount. My little puppy teeth were like needles and when I sank them in, she didn't think yelping at her customers was terribly professional.

Putting us on "mute" only meant she had whole conversations wondering why everyone was ignoring her! – she kept forgetting to "unmute", bless, she's quite dim for a clever person.

At one tele-conference, when Mum was talking, one of her colleagues said "I can hear a parrot" she confessed that it was me running amok with my squeaky hamburger. Eventually, she wrestled me to the ground, separated me from the hamburger and gave me a considerably quieter toy. The minutes of that particular meeting said that I'd made more of a contribution than most folk and should be invited again.

Anyway, I'm getting way ahead of myself.

CHAPTER 10

Dad's talking "dolphin" and Mummy's a Penguin

"When puppies become wild and unruly, it's best to use a nice safe puppy pen. Then when they settle, you can just climb out"

The morning after I arrived home, Mum phoned the vet and said "Remember us? We now have our puppy."

St Francis Veterinary Care took our details over the phone and said to bring me in the following week for my first injection. They wouldn't take me straight away because the shock of leaving my mother, brothers and sisters might all be a bit traumatic. That sometimes manifests itself as diare, diah, dio, erm… runny poo and they needed to give me time to settle in.

So I was booked in the following week.

Off we went to the vet's in my Mum's car. She dropped me and Dad off at the door and went looking for a parking space.

Oh boy, I totally misbehaved. I was used to being handled by Barbara, I didn't have that much contact with men and my Dad is **huge** I wanted my Mum and she had just wandered off…

Dad was embarrassed. He put me on the scales, I was 5.3 kilos and yipping and yelping. Two emergencies had just come in – both dogs with cut paws on glass carelessly thrown into long grass. We hate people who do that.

So we had to wait …bummer.

Then the door opened and Mum came in. I scrambled from Dad to Mum and we sat in the vets, me with my bum in her lap and my chin on her chest. I just gazed up at her and she gazed down at me.

Every now and then she would kiss my nose and I would either lick her or sigh a huge contented sigh. Julie, the Practise Manager (and one of my new best friends) said she didn't know which one of us was most in love…

Julie took my photo for the Newsletter but the first one looked like I was being strangled (I wasn't) so they took another one. Yup, I'm already a celeb.

When the vet came out and said "Fizz Birkett" for some strange reason, it made my Mum and Dad laugh. That was the first time I'd been treated like a real "person" They laugh at weird stuff, I'm used to it now.

We went into a room with a steel table. Dad lifted me onto it and the vet started getting very familiar! Touching my ears, toes, teeth, shining lights in my eyes and even said – "Oh yes, there are two little testicles in there."

When Mum said "Not for long" he covered my ears.

Apparently he stuck a needle in the back of my neck, but I really didn't feel anything and he gave me a treat. A treat is a treat and should never be ignored…my lovely vet often gives me treats – sometimes for no reason at all.

His last words as we left the surgery were "My, what an

impressive pup." I have no idea why my Mum and Dad brimmed with pride at that moment – I mean what had they contributed to my impressiveness?

Mum was really worried about my biting habit.

I'd start chewing gently and sometimes get a bit rough, but the thing that really freaked her out was every now and then, we'd be snuggling up together on my massive new beanbag or we'd be having a little stroll around the garden and for no apparent reason, I'd get this wolf like look in my eye and pounce at her head, hands, feet, anything remotely close and have a really good go at a fully-fledged bite.

I'd do it with Dad too…and the Grannies …and Grandad… and 2 year old Olly.

Their puppy book said to make sure you play enough stimulating games to use up energy. So they'd put yummy cheese inside upside down plastic tubs and I'd have to work out how to get it. I had a ball you could put treats in and I'd nudge it around the house or they'd hide treats in my cage, keeping the door open so I knew I could wander in and out but sometimes, all I really wanted to do was…well, bite them. So the puppy book said:

- **walk away**, so I'd just follow them and bite them anyway,
- **yelp and let him know you're hurt**, that works for an instant then I'd try and bite them again,
- **give him a toy to bite instead**, works best with me, or a doggy chew is good but I'd still try a sly bite now and then,
- **Stand still and shout in a voice loud enough to scare him,** my Mum is useless at shouting. My Dad is good, but

after a while, I just thought, blimey he's "shouty" and went back to biting,

- **Ignore him,** best ever, I could bite as much as I wanted and they did absolutely nothing about it.

So, when they were at the vets, they took the opportunity to ask about the best way to stop me biting. Their advice was to try a high pitched whine, like a dog crying, or growling at me, on the basis that is what Meg would have done if I got too rough.

Worth a try.

The first time my Dad did the high pitched whine, I must say, it was the weirdest noise ever. It certainly stopped me biting for a little while and made my Mum say "Hey Fizz, Dad's talking dolphin…"

Truth is, all puppies go through a "bitey" stage, I mean, hello, we're dogs, so be patient. But you may need to try a few methods to stop biting – and other nasty habits that I'll come to soon.

On day 2, they put a collar on me. Mum had bought it 'specially because it was soft material, so it wouldn't hurt my neck. Not that horrible hard nylon stuff and certainly not chafing leather and besides, the ring thingy for my lead looked nice and strong in case I pulled. **Moi?**

They put it on and I scratched a little bit, but to be honest, every time I scratched with my hind legs, I fell over so it was all a bit pointless. Besides, I was seeing and sniffing loads of new stuff so I wasn't really all that bothered and they decided that even though the puppy book said to just leave it on a couple of hours each day, I just kept it on and pretty much forgot about it.

It wasn't quite so simple with my lead. The first time they put that on, I went **mental.** Instead of introducing me to it immediately and maybe letting me trot around the garden with it gradually when I first came home, they left it a couple of weeks – **big mistake!**

Thing is, my garden at home, at Nana's and at Grandad's are all closed in and I can't escape. At Granny's, there's substantial potential for serious bids for freedom – and I've found most of them.

So they thought it would be a good idea to put a long chain in Granny Midge's garden and try to tie me to it to keep me safe. **I went berserk!** I yipped, yelped, and struggled as if I was being chopped to pieces. I nearly choked myself to death and they took me off the chain – never to put it anywhere near me again. I admit, I'm a bit of a sulky dog and didn't go near them for a couple of hours, well maybe half an hour. Well ok, about 10 minutes. But then I started to grudgingly respond to their pathetic need for Fizzykisses.

So, walks in Granny's garden had to be heavily supervised for a couple of months. Ok by me…

Besides, they decided the chain wasn't all that safe anyway. As soon as I could jump onto the garden seat and sniff next door's garden, I could have leapt over the fence, and at best, gotten tangled in bushes and at worst, I could have hung myself.

I've managed to leap from the seat right into the arms of our

40

startled neighbour a couple of times – she managed to catch me too, she should be a goalie!

Not long after this, when I was able to go walkies, I wrapped my extendable lead (more about these later) several times around my Mum's knees making her walk like a penguin before she plummeted to the ground. Dad wasted no time getting his own back for the "dolphin" jibe…

Licking bird-poo off the rockery - Yum

CHAPTER 11

We've put his life in terrible danger and OMG, we're starving him

"To err is human, to forgive is canine"

When I first came home and pood all over the kitchen floor, Mum and Dad thought I'd be a right handful.

Truth is, I wasn't really that bad.

Barbara put sheets of newspaper in our pen in the barn and Meg showed us that we should poo on that and not to poo in the place we slept.

When Mum and Dad put newspaper in our kitchen I just systematically ripped it to shreds.

So they thought they would buy puppy training pads and put them beside our back door. I hated them and walked around them, being very careful not to put my paws on the stinky surfaces.

From the first night home, I was allowed to roam in our garden, closely supervised for a few weeks and then eventually on my own. They'd walk around the garden with me every hour or so and especially after meals or as soon as I'd woken from a nap. I've mentioned how cold it was and with the door constantly open, the kitchen was like Siberia to my sun loving folks.

They turned into Howard and Hilda with their chunky knit matching sweaters to keep them warm and suffered relentless and cruel taunts from their friends who came to meet me.

Initially, I'd go into the garden and as soon as I pood or peed I'd be told I was a "good boy" and get a puppy treat.

To be fair, it really didn't take all that long for me to realise that I must pee in the garden and not in the house. But just to keep them on their toes, I'd look defiantly in their eyes, adopt the pose and pee in the kitchen – just because I could.

Their coping strategy was to shout "**NO FIZZ**" and stop me mid pee, then lift me into the garden to continue the blissful art of peeing.

There was a temporary blip when Mum was telling Aunty Susan what a "clean" dog I was. Only one poo episode in the house and only a couple of pees. She was positively preening when Aunty Susie uttered words that suddenly turned her blood cold…

"Don't you know you can't let him anywhere outside until he's had his injections?"

Well, I had to revive my Mum with puppy kisses, she was completely distraught to have put my life in such danger. She rang St Francis's immediately and said "I've let my puppy in the garden to pee n' poo am I putting him in danger?"

Luckily, the vet said, "No he's fine. Just don't let him out where **any** old dog can roam around, let him socialise with dogs who are up to date with their injections and for goodness sake **stop worrying so much**"…Never gonna happen.

 43

I was very happy to eat the puppy mush that me and my brothers and sisters were raised on. Barbara said it was ok to mix in a scrambled egg - made with water, no milk – apparently cow's milk is a strict no-no for puppies. **Top Tip:** don't be tempted to buy expensive "puppy milk" from supermarkets, tap water is just fine.

Let me tell you – **Never, ever, ever,** let my Mum cook for you. She's the worst cook in the entire world. Her worst ever dish is scrambled egg.

The only time she made it for me, I trotted into the garden and was promptly sick as a…erm dog!

Puppy mush was ok and when my Dad mixed a scrambled egg in, it was even better but you always remember the first time you were sick and even though my Dad never let Mum near the eggs again she just couldn't help herself interfering.

They had to keep remembering to soak the mush pellets. I soon got into the routine of knowing when it was chow time and got a bit frantic waiting for my mush to be ready if they forgot the soaking bit.

They forgot a lot.

We need four meals a day when we're little – more than when we're fully grown up and try as they might, there was nowhere to go for a comprehensive guide on how much food I should have. All advice seemed to be very general and too wide ranging for the anoraks within to make considered decisions on my food intake. Even the experts; vet, puppy book, Aunty Fee, were vague and cavalier about it all and the

Internet gave them so many options they ended up being more confused than when they'd started.

Then there were the treats to consider. I get treats when I do something good, and let's face it, I'm usually damned good, so they mount up. How soon before a handful of treats amounts to lunch or dinner?

They were really worried that I was getting too much or not enough. They would scrutinise me constantly and say things like:

"I can feel his ribs"
"He's got a fat little belly"
"Does he look hungry to you?"
"He sleeps a lot – is he weak with hunger?"
"He sleeps a lot – have we fed him too much?"

Dad pretended not to worry, but did anyway and Mum became a travel agent for Guilt Trips.

One of the really tricky things about being a puppy is you can't read – sometimes neither can your humans – be prepared for this.

I guess Mum didn't know that Barbara would send such a big bag of puppy mush home with me because, remember the big pile of homecoming stuff I told you my Mum had bought – amongst that somewhere was a big box of "complete" puppy food.

Anyway, she picked this particular brand, not only because it was award winning, was clinically proven to improve your puppy's coat and skin (omega 6 and 3) teeth and bones

 45

(calcium) healthy muscle development (protein) healthy blood (iron) and energy (vitamins and minerals) besides, she liked the colour of the bits and thought I would too. She was warned **not** to change my diet abruptly. If she did, she was to expect trouble.

Dad wanted to just keep me on the mush for a while longer but pretty soon, she was mixing a few bits of my new puppy food with the mush.

Then it would be a handful.

Then it got to the point that I would pick out the new stuff and eat it and leave the mush behind.

Mum got a little smug but that created new anxieties – I have dedicated a whole section to Dog Poo for you to enjoy. But for now, it seemed the mush was redundant and I was weaned on to complete dry puppy food.

So that I wouldn't be a "fussy" eater, they would slice sausage or chicken into my meals. Can you believe you are reading this?

After a few weeks, when I became a very fussy eater, the vet suggested that I wasn't eating properly because they were mixing yummy treats with essential food. He said I had a fundamental right to my meals but really have to work for treats. Bummer!

Anyway, the food quantity thing was really bugging them so they bought a big bag of my new favourite puppy food and read the instructions. I should be getting between 45 grams and 125 grams per day for my weight. An average mug holds about 130 grams.

Which end of the scale was I? They decided to go for the middle, for no other reason than they had no idea where else to go…

Diligently, they would weigh 95 grams of puppy food out and split it into 4 meals. I was getting treats on top of this – thank God, because the **eejits** hadn't read the packet properly.

Dad rang Mum at work and told her they were feeding me the amount for my **puppy weight** when the box quite categorically says "Estimated **adult** weight."

Ever the drama queen, Mum shrieked **"Oh my God, we're starving him."**

So all of a sudden, my food intake rocketed to about 350 grams plus treats. They had absolutely no idea what my Estimated Adult Weight was going to be, so there was a lot of guessing and another frantic call to the vet who suggested I'd be around 20-25kg. In case you're wondering, I seem to have levelled out at 20kg so far.

A couple of times, they desperately stopped me eating my own poo – or anyone else's for that matter. My Mum wondered if I was trying to eat it because they were actually starving me to death…but no, it's yummy. Try it sometime…horse poo is my particular favourite.

For a few days, all was quiet on the food front, when on a routine stroll around, me and Dad met a fellow Collie lover. They got talking and she declared herself horrified that they were feeding me food commercially available in …a…a…a… **Supermarket…** "Are you mad?" she said, "Throw it in the bin and give him proper food" but then she failed to say exactly what "proper food" is. Around the same time, I got a little bored with my new packet food and wouldn't eat it, the panic started all over again…

Mum said I wasn't eating because Dad had called me "fat" one day.

They researched Border Collie puppy food on the internet and it seems there are as many different opinions of what to feed your puppy as there are puppies in the world. Some feel only natural food is appropriate (fresh meat, some vegetables, rice) and say the commercial big boys use the body parts of dead animals that humans would never eat. They think you shouldn't feed your dog anything you wouldn't eat yourself.

Others, some including well respected dog clubs, recommend you let the dog food specialists do their job and provide nutritionally balanced grub for dogs. Each meal will then contain the right amounts of protein, calcium, vitamins, omega 3and 6 and all the other stuff they need to stay healthy. But also said, it may be incredibly boring over time.

They recommend the more expensive commercial stuff on the basis it is likely to be better than the cheap stuff – but there doesn't seem to be any evidence available to substantiate this.

Most seem to agree that certain cereals such as maize and soya beans are a strict no-go area.

As you can imagine, the parents went into a frenzy. Off we all went to our local pet shop and read every damned packet of every damned dog food in the whole place. The assistants are lovely and always make me welcome and gave us lots of advice about nutrition.

48

We left with a wet food guaranteed to contain fresh lamb, turkey, chicken and beef , which they mixed with a new "complete" food. *Top Tip: If the packet doesn't say "complete" food then it isn't! Mix it with a complete food to make it fit the bill.*

We also bought another – and ridiculously expensive- complete puppy food they would gradually replace my normal food and mix it in with the meaty stuff to make sure I got everything I needed.

The wet food has now gone the journey and after trying pretty much every complete dry food on the market I'm on a healthy, well balanced, well respected – if a little expensive, dry food. I like it, my coat is fabulously glossy, my eyes are bright and my nose is cold and wet, so that's all that matters until my Mum starts interfering again…

In spite of the fact that the idiots tried to starve me, feed me all the wrong things and vary my diet against everyone's advice, I continue to thrive as a puppy.

Somebody pass my chewy, I'm starvin'

CHAPTER 12

Fizz stinks and he has a bare behind

"Never wrestle in a field with a Collie, you both get dirty and the Collie loves it"

On my second day home, my Mum just had to say what had been pretty obvious but so far, left unsaid – even by the pristine Nana Tosh…

"Fizz stinks"

My Dad was really annoyed at this unnecessary outburst and said I was a dog and therefore had a God given right to smell of dog.

When it comes to dirt, me and Dad are on the same wavelength. He doesn't mind when I eat soil out of the plant pots or when I lick bird poo off the rockery but Mum goes berserk and chases me to prise my jaws open and remove rocks, old leaves, plastic bags, glass, rusty nails, dead seagull, dried frog and anything else that takes my fancy.

I love my Dad.

"No, it's more than that, he really honks to high heaven."

She asked Nana Tosh, who agreed "I love him to bits, but he's stinging my eyes with that smell."

So, once again, poor old St Francis's had Mum on the phone saying "I really don't mean to be a fussy pet owner (!) but my puppy stinks. How soon can I bathe him?"

They explained that in the litter, especially at first, the puppies would be rolling in all sorts and the smell would be comforting, but it was ok to bathe me in a little luke warm water using a small amount of baby shampoo and to avoid my head. They shouldn't bathe me too often because my coat has natural oils and the nurse doesn't recommend the dry shampoo in case of irritation. They told them to groom me regularly, preferably when I'm sleepy or I'd probably try to chew the brush (**probably!**)

Let me tell you, I **hated** it.

They stuck me in the sink and I sat in about three inches of warm water until Mum shampooed and rinsed me. I'd never looked so miserable in my whole nine weeks of life and wasn't sure I'd forgive them for this…**ever.**

To be honest, they made it mercifully brief. I have my own set of lovely fluffy towels, their cast offs, I suspect and Dad lifted me out of the water to freedom. I wriggled, squirmed and shook myself frantically. I got a fair amount of water all over the kitchen and drenched Mum and Dad. A puppy soaked in three inches of water can send a surprising amount of splashes into all directions – they'd be finding them for weeks and frankly, it serves them right.

Eventually I settled into puppy cuddles on Dad's lap, I dried surprisingly quickly but he had a very suspicious looking damp patch in his jeans. If this continues, Mum will whip him off to the vet…

In all fairness, from that point on, I was pretty much irresistible.

I have a gorgeously soft and fluffy coat which has a delicious puppy smell to it, huge hazel eyes and when someone remarked about my cute "blotchy" nose, Mum corrected them with a rather sharp "I think you'll find they're beauty spots" response.

After a few weeks my beauty spots all joined up and by 14 weeks, I had a grey muzzle. I was the oldest looking puppy you've ever seen. Mum wondered if they should have called me Benjamin Button Biscuit Birkett?

I'd become so fluffy that you can imagine my surprise when I was playing in the garden one day and Dad said "Fizz has a bare behind."

"No he hasn't, he's fluffy."

"Not a bare behind, a bear behind, as in - he looks like a bear from behind."

They were at it again…

You smell funny, but I think I'll keep you…

CHAPTER 13

From Prada to Pet Shops and Poo Mania

"Whenever you observe an animal closely, you feel as if a human being sitting inside were making fun of you"

Every day, I seem to be learning something new and exciting and Mum and Dad are keen for me to meet lots of people and their pets.

Dad has been invited round to visit people he's never been invited round to visit before just so I could meet their precious pooches.

My second visit to the vet's was two weeks after the first. Everyone was amazed at how much I'd grown and whilst I'd been trained (aka, bribed with tasty treats to do what the humans wanted) to "sit" I wouldn't when Dad put me on the scales.

I was roughly 6.9 kilos and in a wriggly, excited state because there were other dogs in the surgery. They wouldn't let me on the floor or anywhere near the other dogs because I still needed my second injection – bummer.

The vet this time was bubbly, noisy and frankly a little mad – in a nice, friendly way. She made Dad hold me, made a big fuss of me, told us she was sneaking up behind me and then she jabbed me without any of us knowing what had just happened.

Mum asked about my weight and was I growing normally? She said there was nothing to worry about, I was a healthy and contented puppy. It didn't do anything to relieve Mum's guilt for starving me but she didn't 'fess up either!

I had to wait another two weeks before I could go out and I was becoming a little stir crazy.

For a little boy, I can cover quite a bit of ground and can sneak into the most unexpected places if they don't keep a close eye on me. One day, I was found in the cupboard where we keep our leads, poo bags, coats and boots. Mum keeps her work stuff in there too and I regularly go in for the odd chewing session.

One day at work, she noticed her beautiful dove grey, soft leather, Prada bag had an "A" missing and was now declaring itself a "Prad" bag. She wasn't happy but she couldn't pin it on me Guv! She did, however, watch my poo very closely for a few days!

No change there…

My Mum is obsessed by my poo. She was worried that it was too runny before I went to the vet and thought they wouldn't inject me and that would put my puppy school back. She worries if it's too soft, too hard, too little. She has poo bags in every coat pocket and up the sleeves of all her jumpers.

She "packages" the poo bags so that the bin men don't know what they are (would they care?)

She worries that if I don't poo when I go out and they have to

put me in my cage at night, that I'll be in terrible pain holding it in. I am proud to say, I have never pood or peed in my bed – well would you?

She speaks to Dad every morning and every evening when I'm not at home to find out if I've pood.

There was a time when I thought my name was Hazzi Haddapoo?

She checks the consistency every time and really has no idea what consistency it should be, but she compares it to human poo. Gross or what? That doesn't deter her from observing – out loud – that the firm ones are much nicer to pick up than the runny ones.

As I said…The woman is obsessed and needs a hobby.

Because of my fondness for soil, poo, twigs, plants, rocks and pretty much anything else I fancy eating, my puppy poo was never consistent. In a single "sitting" I can drop it in about 3 or 4 places in the garden. They scoop it up immediately, but have to walk around to find it. They are often guided by the highly pungent aroma. I feel it's important to keep your humans' minds agile.

From a very early age, I knew I could poo in the garden. Our garden, Nana's garden, Granny's garden, Grandad's garden, anyone's garden really. I knew that because every time I did it, I got treats, lovely cuddles, tickled ears and told I was a "good boy" in a silly baby voice.

Also from an early age, I knew I mustn't pee or poo in the house. When I did that, I got a very stern "naughty boy" voice

55

and if they caught me in time, they'd shout to stop me, pick me up gently and put me outside.

Every now and then, for a few weeks and for no other reason than I could, I would have a little accident now and then.

Most of the time, I'd try to tell them but they didn't understand. I mean, I'd bark at a door (how was I to know it was a cupboard? I just knew I needed a door to open and be let out) but sometimes, I'd look them in the eye and just pee on the kitchen floor for the hell of it.

Once I started walking outside, I didn't realise I could pee and poo there too. I'd sniff every blade of grass, lamp post, even the dog poo bins and it didn't occur to me that I had permission to pee n' poo anywhere else but the gardens.

People told them they should have said the words "pee" and "poo" every time I, well, erm, peed or pood in the garden and I would have known when I went outside that it was ok. Because of this severe neglect, It took me ages to "do it" outside of the garden. Even when they waved poo bags at me saying "It's ok Fizz, you can poo, we have bags" I couldn't be persuaded.

The first time I pood outside, Mum told me I was a "good boy", gave me a treat then to my absolute horror, started dancing around it. She was trying to demonstrate that it was fine and they wanted me to do it outside but the embarrassment was so shocking that I didn't do it again for ages. I mean, for pity's sake, there was a well hard looking Husky watching...

To help me out here, Mum told Dad he'd have to cock his leg

against a lamp post and show me how it's done. She also said any "proper" Dad would poo on the grass until I got the hang of it. He wasn't keen, besides, he'd need considerably bigger poo bags.

After some time, I pood outside again, in a field beside our house. Mum wasn't paying enough attention to where I'd "dropped" it and picked up a carrier bag full before she found the warm one...

My Mum and Dad get really angry with irresponsible people who don't pick up poo after their pets. I mean, it's totally unfair to leave it for men, women, children and other animals to walk in. They get quite passionate about it. They get especially annoyed when people take the time and trouble to pick it up then drop the blinking bags on the ground. What's the point of that then?

Uncle Andy said he sometimes leaves bags of his Labrador Sam's poo under a bush if there are no bins along his walk, then he picks it up and disposes of it on his way back. Mum wasn't impressed. "For goodness sake Andy, swing your poo with pride. People will know you're a responsible dog owner and you might even encourage serious dog poo dodgers to do the right thing and pick it up."

Aunty Fee reckons that just like humans don't care much for public toilets, then neither do I. I can go for a 2 hour walk and still come home and poo in the comfort of my own garden.

I quite like pooing on my Nana's patio. She comes out with buckets of water to clean it and we have great fun, usually resulting in both of us getting soaking wet. One time she missed a bit so I helped her out by licking it all up when she wasn't looking then followed her into the house and licked her face. Mum witnessed the whole thing but decided not to tell.

When Nana bought a garden hose, to cope with my patio/poo habit, I chewed a few holes in it. It's much better now.

At one time, Mum couldn't pass a clothes shop without having a sneaky look. She's like that with pet shops now.

I have dozens of toys, have tried every puppy treat known to man or should I say, dog and have gadgets they haven't quite worked out how to use yet.

I'm on to my second fluffy bed at both home and at Granny's. Mum even bought a "Coop Cup" to hang on my cage to stop me sitting in my water bowl. Well frankly, I liked sitting in my water bowl.

I have an equally large number of gadgets, toys and bedding at Nana's and at Grandad's.

And all I really need is my plant pot… I can throw it in the air and catch it but they have never been quick enough with the camera to prove it when they brag to their friends.

I kind of know which toys are mine, so when I split my red tennis ball and Dad thought it would be good fun to stick it on his nose like a clown, why was he so surprised that I lunged at him and tried to rip off his face to retrieve my ball?

In a short space of time, Mum has become the world's expert on hide chews. Round ones, cigar shaped, thin flats, bone shapes, boot shapes and can spend ridiculous amounts of time

perusing the shelves for different types. That said, I do love them and they stop me chewing furniture and people.

She took me and Granny to the pet shop to show us the lovely hide chews. Turning to Granny, she asked "Have you got any flat chews at home?" and Granny replied "Do you mean sandals?"

They're all at it now…

Me and my plant pot

CHAPTER 14

The Big Weekend: Walkies, Puppy School and Chips

*"No-one appreciates the sheer genius of your conversation
like a dog does"*

At first, whenever we went out anywhere, Mum or Dad would lift me out of the car and carry me to the next place we were headed. I didn't question any of that. I'd just sniff whatever I could and enjoy the scenery from my vantage point.

Two weeks after my second injection, on 13th March, it was safe for me to go out into the big wide world.

I had no idea that day that Mum and Dad woke up in an extreme state of excitement. I mean they wanted a dog to walk and here I was baby…

Today was the big day.

My very first walk.

They put my lead on, which I still hated, until they opened the door and I trotted out to a whole new world of sights, noises and new stuff to sniff.

Another thing people will tell you, is that little puppies don't need a lot of exercise at first. We have new little paws and

growing bones and muscles. But really, how long is a short walk? We started with a short walk from home, through the estate, across a busy main road and then through Nana's estate and back. This was a ten minute walk for anyone used to doing this kind of thing. It took us 45 minutes. I had to sniff absolutely everything. But as I've said, I didn't pee or poo whilst I was out.

Entering the world of dog owners means my parents have become part of a strange and mysterious parallel universe where human identity ceases to exist. We go walkies and meet Fudge's Dad and Maddie's Mum. None of these people have their own names, they are known only by their dogs' names.

It's a world where talking about dog poo is perfectly acceptable, nay, expected!

People tell us what grooming tools they prefer, where to get the cheapest poo bags, where all the great walks are, which hotels accept pets, the doggie list goes on. There are very few "human" exchanges like "hello, how are you today, that's a very fetching Parka" It's all "dog talk"

When Aunty Dawn came to see me she made Mum smile when she said to me "Can you smell my Daisy?" so now Mum always greets dogs by asking "Can you smell my Fizz?" Uncle Barry is worse, when he takes his Springer Spaniel to the groomers, he tells everyone he's got a baldy Charlie. Please, may they grow out of this … soon.

Dog people are generally really nice and friendly and don't mind at all when I go charging towards them and their dogs. They understand that I'm a puppy and give me lots of tickles.

They tell me which of their dogs are friendly and which ones to steer clear of. I ignore all of that and have been growled at and nipped a couple of times. Nothing serious, just the older guys telling me I'm getting on their nerves. I back off and go and get my Dad when I feel threatened.

Most dog lovers are notoriously generous, often loopy and incredibly devoted when it comes to their pets. Let me give you a couple of examples:

We live beside a beautiful stretch of beach. There's a purpose built walkway running alongside. Every day, a man walks his Great Dane along that walkway and he carries a stylish footstool across his shoulders. It's a beautiful stool with mahogany Queen Anne legs and a plush red velvet seat. We thought maybe he understood the need for his dog to have a good run, but perhaps the man himself suffered with some mobility problems. But no. Every few hundred yards, he puts the stool on the ground, the dog sits on it and puts his head on the man's waist and gets his ears tickled until he's ready to resume the walk. Mum told the man his dog had better furniture than us! He just smiled and said "He loves this beach, but we're old boys now and he gets a bit tired."

When Uncle Barry and Aunty Jules take Charlie to the beach, they stroll along the sand and at a certain point, Charlie runs up into the dunes. He stands there on that spot and drops his ball down to them. They run around the beach retrieving the ball and throw it back up to him. It's a refreshing twist to a game of "fetch" and they don't see anything weird about that picture.

My next walk, the same day, was on the beach for about half an hour. I have really keen hearing. Noises tend to freak me

out until I become used to them, so the screechy seagulls and crashing waves were a bit scary, but the parents were ridiculously ecstatic that we were finally walking on their beloved beach that I soon got used to it all.

They kept me on a short lead for the first couple of days but it seemed a bit rubbish to be on the beach and not able to romp. They daren't let me off the lead because other people and their dogs were far more interesting and I wasn't guaranteed to come back.

Nana Tosh bought me an extendable lead. There are many different opinions of these, mainly:

They're dangerous:
- They get wrapped around people, trees, bushes, other dogs and can strangle me if my parents don't pay attention
- If I run at full pelt further than the rope will take me, I'll get a very nasty yank that sends me tumbling and can hurt my neck
- They wrap around my legs, trip me up and hurt me
- They give humans a nasty rope burn if they are holding the ropey bit trying to stop me hurtling into unsuspecting cyclists

They're a Godsend:
- They let me roam and sniff in the woods and beach at a safe distance
- They have a locking mechanism so the parents control how far I can go. Short lead for busy roads, long lead for fields and beaches
- They can teach me to catch, fetch and drop my ball with no fear that I'll be able to take off when another dog comes on the scene

- They can teach me "recall" without letting me off the lead in busy places where distractions happen
- I soon learned how far I could romp before the lead would run out so the nasty yanking only happened when I did it deliberately

The parents decided on the Godsend approach and whilst it's true that I have indeed wrapped my extendable lead around myself, other humans, dogs, trees and have tried to garrotte myself and a wide variety of other species, it has given me lots more freedom and provided a degree of peace of mind for the control freak parents.

Only one person has ever told my Mum to "Get your dog under control" then relented when she saw I was a "baby". Mum blamed a malfunction on the lead locking device. My big hairy bum! She didn't reel me in and lock it in time, it was a Mummy malfunction more like…

My first week at puppy school was great. We met the puppies outside before the class began:

Ben is a German Shepherd cross, born in a shelter to a stray Mum. No one knows who his Dad is but he certainly has Rottweiler in him. I like Ben, he's big, boisterous, noisy and a little bit naughty. He growled at me sometimes but he was my best friend at puppy school.

Blake is a tiny Patterdale Terrier. A lot of his fur had fallen out and he looked like a little old man with a wrinkly brow. His Mum seemed really embarrassed and kept telling us he wasn't contagious. Actually, I didn't care.

Skye is a tiny Springer Spaniel with the most beautiful face, all of us dogs and our humans loved her.

Nemmy is a stunning chocolate Labrador. She liked people much more than she liked us puppies. She looks like butter wouldn't melt but her owners are worried about her biting. Sounds familiar.

Oscar is a gorgeous little Bishon Frise, very cutsie and not at all scared of the big boys (me and Ben).

Then we went inside. There are three instructors:

- June, who leads the class and scans the group looking for social issues and advises us how to deal with them;
- Eileen, the teaching assistant who provides 1 to1 attention for the naughty puppies. I knew early on that me, Eileen and Ben were gonna be buddies;
- Moll who also teaches and does all the admin stuff and helps out in class giving advice and support.

Puppy classes are private and must be paid for, but let me tell you, the value for money and ratio of puppies to trainers is far better than any public school you might put your children through....just a thought.

We met Moll first and she knew who I was immediately from the enrolment forms. She greeted us with "Hello, this must be Fizz."

See what I mean, dog people just don't acknowledge the existence of humans. People exist through their dogs – weird. Nevertheless, my folks were really impressed that we'd never met and she already knew me.

June is very matter of fact and very funny and very sensible. When she talks, Mums and Dads listen and realise they have sometimes been a bit:

- silly,
- over anxious,
- impatient, and
- a whole load of other unattractive human traits.

In a short space of time, she made the parents realise that some of the stuff they were really anxious about was just normal dog behaviour. All puppies bite, chew, bark and ignore people, whenever they feel like it. She told us:

- **Never** hit your puppy, it encourages bad behaviour. I was hoping at this point that Mum and Dad were squirming in shame. They'd tapped my bum a couple of times. Never enough to hurt me, just in an effort to stop me in my tracks. They never did it again;
- **All puppies** try to chew and bite you. They need to learn that gentle chewing with no force is ok, but a hard bite is not. It's very important to learn this when we have our needle sharp baby teeth and not when we have our big boy dangerous teeth;
- **Never** put your puppy into their cage in anger. But if a puppy is misbehaving, put them in the cage for some "time out" for five minutes or until they settle. This is a sensible precaution when you are dangerously close to throttling your pup;
- Keep your living area **calm.** Aggression rubs off.

Then we learned how to sit, stand and lie down. June says that we have to have treats that represent "delicious yumminess" so that we **really** want to work for them. That's not boring dog biscuits or even doggie treats, but "human grade" treats like cooked liver, sausage, cheese, hot dogs. **Top tip:** leave these treats whole then break off a toe pad sized piece every time we do well. Otherwise, sausage and liver go to crumbs and cheese goes to mushy stuff – plus, we can always see there's more if we can only just figure out what we have to do to get it.

Anyway, puppy treats can be expensive. A packet of "own brand" supermarket sausages or a slab of liver cost a fraction of the price and last a lot longer. If you're sly like my Dad, you can sneak a sausage in your pocket for yourself now and again.

Basic training (for the purposes of the exercise, we'll refer to all pups as "he or him" No offence to girlie pups!)

To **sit**, you place a yummy treat just above the head, between the nose and eyes, your puppy's head goes back to get the treat and his bum goes to the floor. When the bum is on the floor, say "Sit" and give him the treat.

To **stand**, put the yummy treat above the nose and slowly bring it upwards until your pup is standing. Say "Stand" and give him the treat.

To **lie down**, put the treat in your clenched hand on the floor, the pup will try to retrieve it by lying down, say "Down" and give him the treat when he lies down.

To **stay**, get the pup to sit. Let him know you have a treat in one hand and back away with the flat palm of

your other hand facing him. Tell him to "stay" then say "come" and wave the treat at him. Give him the treat and walk further away each time he gets it right.

To **heel**, put a lead on the pup. Hold the strap in your left hand and take up the slack in your right hand. The pup will walk on this shortened lead on your right hand side (reverse this if you're left handed) Hold a yummy treat close to his nose in your right hand. After short distances, give him the treat and gradually increase the distance between treats.

To **recall**, make it inviting for him to come to you. Why would he want to come to you if you resort to shouting? Kneel down and say "come on then (name of pup) come see" in a welcoming voice. Shake a toy, or have a treat handy. Some pups respond to a tin with beans in to rattle at them. Basically, find the thing that he really wants and use this to get him to come to you. Use his name so he gets used to it and eventually he will know what you want when you call his name. Reward with yummy treats when he gets it right.

After each successful attempt, as you're giving the treat, give lots of praise. Repeat each one a gazillion times. Easy peasy.

Homework was set and we had to practice sit, stand and lie down in no particular order for next week.

Being the perfect pup, amongst all this excitement, I had somehow arranged to get my Mum a Mother's day card and a box of chocs. She was **ridiculously** ecstatic.

 68

Next day, Dad went to work and left me with Mum and Granny. Apparently, I was getting my microchip – whatever that was. The great thing is, not only was I allowed to walk to the vets, I could scramble around the floor with the other dogs. The nurse called my name "Fizz Birkett" and in we went, back to the room with the steel table. I was quite happy about that, this is the place I get biscuits and cuddles for doing absolutely nothing.

Our vets don't want me to be nervous about visiting so they said we can call in at any time. I can get weighed or we can have puppy cuddles or even just a chat.

Now, I had no idea that Mum hadn't slept the night before, worrying that the microchip needle was a bit of a big beastie.

Dad didn't sleep either because he couldn't come with me. He made Mum promise to ring when "it was done."

The nurse examined my bones, muscles, ears, eyes, nose, paws and before I knew it, she'd stuck the microchip between my shoulder blades. No dramas as our antipodean cousins would say. Mum was relieved and rang Dad straight away to stop him worrying.

Nursey confirmed that my folks should check daily;

- my paws, **gently** feeling in between toes and pads,
- my ears, **gently** washing inside with a damp (not wet) cloth and never using cotton buds,
- my tail, lifting it **gently** and checking all was well. Yuk, Yuk and double Yuk!
- My muscles and bones, running their hands around me to make sure all was well - guess how – **gently, but firmly** of course!

69

And asked if Mum had any questions. Boy, did she regret that one!

Q: How much food should I give him?
A: Well follow the instructions on the box and go for something around the middle of the range they give you. Don't forget, he's getting lots of treats whilst you are training him so top of the range would be too much, he's a big pup so bottom of the range wouldn't be enough.

Q: But how do I know what his estimated adult weight is?
A: We can't be exact but I'd say he'll reach around the 20kg mark. Use that as a guide.

Q: What's the best food for him?
A: I'll give you a sample of the one we recommend but he looks fine on what you are feeding him.

On and on she went and the nurse patiently answered all of her questions.

When she started to mention brushing, Mum jumped the gun and said "I know we should brush him, but he hates it."

Nursey shocked her even further by saying, "I'm talking about brushing his teeth. Start when he's young and he'll just accept it."

Mum left the vets with a dog toothbrush that you attach as a finger brush thingy and some dog toothpaste. Actually, I love it. I think it's a game and Mum/Dad brush my teeth in the hope I won't suffer with bad teeth and need expensive dental work when I'm older.

Many of Mum and Dad's friends think they have now gone completely nuts. Mum's friend Lily said "a dog toothbrush, dog toothpaste!! What do they do in the wild?"

Cool as a biscuit, Mum said "have you ever smelled a wild dog's breath?"

She hadn't. End of...

Hiding my dignity from Mum and her blimmin' camera!

CHAPTER 15

Chasing cars and going bald

" Don't take life too seriously, no-one gets out alive"

I really don't like cars much.

When we had that really long journey from Yorkshire, I was no bother. But I was tiny and just wanted to sleep.

My next long journey was from Home to Granny's, to get me settled in for the first time.

A friend told Dad, "Take the parcel shelf off and make him comfy in the boot. It might be an idea to get one of those grille things for the back seat?"

So they packed all their gear onto the back seat, put a lovely comfy pillow, some toys and treats and chews in the boot, put two thick rugs over the tops of the back seats so I couldn't scratch them and satisfied themselves that, although they hadn't got round to getting the grille, it was light and airy and I couldn't get over the top, so I'd be safe, secure and comfy.

WRONG!!

Dad was so smug about how comfy he'd made the boot that he joked he wanted to get in and lie down himself. "Well go right ahead Mister"! I thought, "Because let me assure you, I ain't staying there for long".

They lifted me in and I yipped and yelped as soon as the car got off the drive. I made that last for ages. They ignored me.

I cried pathetically and whimpered. That **always** gets to them but they ignored that too. Mmmmm, this was going to be harder than I thought.

So I scratched and scrabbled around a bit. That got their attention. Dad shouted something and I gave him a bit of his own medicine and ignored him.

Scratching and scrabbling meant that after a while I was able to manoeuvre my pillow to form a small mound big enough to allow me to squeeze through the narrow gap at the top of the seat.

If you have never heard a grown man scream in blind panic, let me tell you - it's ugly.

"He's oot" was Dad's bloodcurdling cry!

Mum was driving on a busy dual carriageway with nowhere to stop safely and it's fair to say they were almost wearing brown trousers they certainly hadn't left home in.

They were worried that I'd somehow crawl to them and impede Mum's driving and we'd all be killed in a 10 car pile-up.

The truth is – when they were finally able to stop safely, I was nestled on the back seat with my head contentedly resting on a still warm, cooked chicken. Mmmmmmmm, blissssssss. The chicken was in a plastic bag so I couldn't really enjoy anything other than the delicious smell but at least I spent the

rest of the journey on Dad's knee, where I belonged. I sincerely hoped they didn't try any of that boot nonsense again in the future.

No such luck. Next time they let me sit on the back seat, but strapped me to the seatbelt with some contraption. They left it too loose and I spent the whole journey with my nose in Mum's armpit. Well, if I was going to hate every minute of it, so was she.

Sadly they cottoned on and I was secured to the seatbelt and able to move around, but not able to get in their way when either of them was driving.

I was once horribly car sick, so I never have any food before a long journey now. I hate cars!

For absolutely no good reason whatsoever, during my second week of walkies, I started chasing after them. I was especially frenzied at night when the lights were on – and the bigger and noisier they were, the worse I'd become.

This was a **very** scary time for the parents. If ever I got loose or broke my lead, I'd be one dead dog. They bought a second collar and lead and doubled them up in case one broke.

They asked what they should do at puppy school. June had absolutely no hesitation:

"Head collar."

"What's one of those?"

"It goes round his neck like a normal collar and has a loop to go around his nose. It's gentle and gives you more control. Pull the collar towards you sharply when he chases cars and say **"No"** in a very sharp and loud voice."

So they got one. Moll fitted it on me, she told us you have to be careful with all collars, check they are not too tight and not so slack that they pull over my ears and come off – you should be able to place 2 slender Mummy fingers between me and the collar or one fat Daddy finger. You have to make sure the loop doesn't go over the soft part of my nose or across my eyes because that would be really uncomfortable. I could still bark, drink and take treats. June suggested they walk me along busy roads and around supermarket car parks to get me so used to cars and people that I'd eventually just ignore them.

But I **really, really** hated the new collar. I squirmed and rolled around the floor yelping and trying to get it off with my paws. Nana and Grandad came to puppy school with us. June encourages the family to come along because they all need to learn how to behave properly around us dogs, Granny's been too. With all the fuss I was making, I swear, there were tears in Nana's eyes.

Thankfully, they took the horrible collar off and it was a quiet drive home.

A shame really, because I'd been a really good pupil that week. We'd practiced sit, stand and down all week and I was perfect.

June even said, it was ok for those who couldn't quite manage it yet, but wasn't at all surprised that I'd got it.

When it was time for me and Dad to go to Granny's, Mum hid the head collar. In all fairness, Dad didn't try too hard to

look for it but played the hard man saying "If it keeps him safe, he'll have to get used to it."

After we left, Mum read the instructions on the box and to be absolutely honest, they are a good idea for helping to control your dog when you have a problem and she started feeling really bad that once again, she may have put my life in extreme danger.

So she rang Aunty Fee. "He's chasing cars."

"You have to stop him, that is sooooooo dangerous."

"I know, but he hates his head collar."

"Try pulling his normal lead sharply towards you and saying "**No**" like June has suggested or try the "**leave it**" command, again in a sharp loud voice so he knows he's doing wrong. Try a tin with some beans in it or a squeaky toy to startle him. Reward him when he gets it right. Walk him around busy roads until he just ignores cars"

So we did.

And within a very hard and worrying week, it worked. Hurrah, am once again Fizz the wonder dog!

But it worked so well, that I started to lie down when we passed a car or a bus so walks started to take considerably longer than they really needed to for a few weeks!

Still, it's better than being squished!

I still chase cyclists and small children though…a dog's gotta have some fun!

 76

Dad tries to instil some discipline into my life. He's always telling Mum that she's "too soft." Every time my Mum asks for Fizz kisses, I sit and put my head up towards her, gaze into her face, then lick her to within an inch of her life. Dad rolls his eyes in utter despair.

One day, me and Dad were playing in the garden when Mum was busy in the house. Little did he know that just as he was tickling me saying "Where's my gorgeous little doggy woggy?" she came out into the garden and caught him.

"That was a private conversation" he sniffed. Better than that though, he was kissing my paws one day, then we went out for a little stroll around the garden. There in the middle of the lawn, was a big lump of Fizzpoo with a perfect paw print right in the middle of it. You can decide who's the softest, or is that daftest?

We'd had a really rotten winter and spring seemed to be a long time in showing its face. Weather wise, Easter was a nightmare and our small garden had become a swamp. Our cream kitchen floor was now continuously mud coloured. Mum and Dad tried valiantly to keep it clean, but it was a lost cause.

Around April, when the weather started behaving a little better, we kept finding big clumps of black hair all over the place. Then the parents noticed that I couldn't stop scratching and once again, the three of us trotted, smartish, off to the vet.

"He's got some horrible skin disease" said Mum "and he'll end up bald."

"Ok, lets scan him" said the nurse, then "nope, he's fine."

"Eh? How can he be fine, I'm finding big clumps of dog hair all over the house?"

"He's a Collie, so he has a double coat."

"Yessssss."

"That means he's shedding his winter coat. Just groom him every day. You might want to take him for specialist grooming where they "blast" his old hair off with a cold hairdryer type contraption. You do this twice a year, once in spring and once in winter. But really, a proper comb and brush will do the trick."

As she normally does, Mum only heard the bits she wanted to and trips to the grooming parlour really appealed. She started dreaming of me having a trim and blow dry and maybe getting my nails done whilst I was there…

Dad was gutted, especially as he thought I'd hate the hairdryer bit and started the brushing regime immediately. I mean, the nerve. He doesn't comb his own hair, he's not getting anywhere near mine, so I made it particularly difficult by squirming and biting the brush. And hey, if Dad's hands got in the way of my teeth, not my fault, ok?

Every day, they brush my entire coat, taking particular care with my "trousers" my tail and my "feathers" (backs of my front legs). It only takes a few minutes and whilst I'm not very keen, I get lovely treats before and after so my protestations are pretty superficial.

We're not too sure how often my nails should be clipped, but I get loads of walks on the pavements and on the beach and

so far they seem fine. There are contraptions that you can buy to clip dog nails but they can be dangerous and very painful if you don't do it properly. ***Top tip:*** *Vets or groomers will do it quite cheaply and properly.*

Our vet's nurse checks mine when we pop in for flea or worm treatments.

That floor ain't gonna stay cream for long!

CHAPTER 16

Fizz the babe magnet and I fight like a cat

*Is there a dog tooth fairy – and if there is, instead of money,
does she leave a dog tooth cheque?*

When I was about 15 weeks old a few things started to change. My teeth started falling out, my bark got a little deeper, I occasionally tried to hump Dad's head and the strangest thing was, I started going behind the bushes at home for a poo.

Mum wondered if maybe I was turning a bit shy?

That idea got smashed to small smithereens when the following weekend, they went for tea to Aunty Sandra's and just as all eleven of them sat down and started tucking in, I appeared in the garden, at the patio doors, in full view of the horrified diners and did a massive poo right in front of them.

Shy, my big brown eye!

Embarrassing episodes apart, socialisation is the most important thing you should do with your puppy.

Let us meet all sorts of people, other dogs and other species. For new pups, busy car parks are great to get used to cars, people of all shapes and sizes and walking past schools and parks at busy times are good for us to get used to shrieking children.

Mum and Dad always put me on a short lead so they can keep control. Most people are really nice and come and give me a cuddle. I get so excited when that happens that I almost wriggle myself into the ground.

I used to just lurrrve other dogs and found them hard to resist. I would always trot over to them and have a sniff. I generally ignore them now, especially if I have a toy to chase but Mum and Dad keep a keen eye out and if an approaching dog is on a lead, they put my lead on. It's possible that the dog or the owner is aggressive. One woman told us she keeps her dog on a lead because he loves people but hates dogs. It's pretty much the opposite in our house!

If approaching dogs don't have a lead on, then it generally but not always, means their owners trust them to recall properly. These folks didn't seem to mind so much when I was a nuisance and wriggled around them. Over time, we realised that I'm much more motivated by my ball or my squeaky than food so they just need to throw something for me to chase to get my attention.

Some people just ignored me, I'd still try and trot over to them. I mean, how could they fail to love me if they'd only take the time to meet me?

So that I could meet more of my family, I went to my Uncle Barney's funeral. After the service, there was a small reception in our local pub and when we left, there were some very attractive, if scantily clad, young women outside. They came straight over and started cooing and fussing over me. Dad was beaming, especially when they bent down to tickle me, revealing their lady bumps.

He stood and chatted for a while and let them play with me, they were telling me all the while how cute I was. I swear, I enjoyed this almost as much as Dad.

Mum watched with amusement from a short distance until we tore ourselves away and joined her. This type of thing happens a lot. My favourite episode was at the pet shop when a very well-endowed young lady bent over me and said "My! what a lovely puppy" Dad was about to compliment her on her lovely puppies when Mum whisked him out of the shop.

They really had no idea what a babe magnet I'd be. Yeah baby…

It's glaringly obvious that I'm a lover not a fighter. My very first aggressive encounter was with my cousin Korky, Granny Midge's cat. She'd lived with Granny for 14 years and she was good mates with Uncle Neil's Labrador, Harvey because they'd grown up together. As a tiny puppy, I had no concept of discretion. I thought everyone should love me and want to meet me so I wriggled up to everyone and everything I saw, getting under feet and paws and generally annoying Korky.

I'd go up and try to sniff her and she'd bat me away with a paw. So, I'd do it again. She'd bat me a bit harder. So, I'd do it again. She'd bat me even harder. This would carry on until I really bugged the living daylights out of her and she'd fly at me "cat-screeching" and I'd run for cover. One day, I bugged her so much, she flew at me, dug her claws in my nose and I ran out of the house with a screaming cat dangling from my nostrils!

Eventually, we learned to circle each other warily and sadly, she died a few months later. Korky's legacy remains however,

because I now fight like a cat. I'm not in the slightest bit aggressive so if I'm threatened in any way, I usually back off or adopt the submissive pose, where I lie on my back and cycle with my paws. This makes Dad curl up in embarrassment, but now and again, I'll sit down and bat my attacker with a paw, Korky style.

Mum, ring the vet, I've lost an ear…

CHAPTER 17

Lumps, bumps and fleeing my abusers

"The reason a dog has so many friends is because he wags his tail instead of his tongue"

I'm a bit accident prone.

When I was tiny, I used to wriggle a lot. One day, I was nestled comfortably in Dad's arms as he was standing in our kitchen. You know our kitchen, the one with the very hard tiled floor; when without any warning, I decided to test my flying skills.

I'm actually rubbish at flying and the world stood still as I leaped from Dad's arms and nosedived towards that hard surface. Mum was screaming, when cool as a biscuit, Dad's goal keeping skills kicked in and he caught me millimetres from smashing my face against the floor.

Never assume we'll be calm at all times, always have total control especially when we're lulling you into a false sense of security licking your face one minute, because as sure as eggs is eggs, the next minute we'll go and test your reflexes.

Many's the time I've raced around the kitchen, slipped on something wet (oops, that might have been me!) and hit my head. All this head banging led the parents to believe I may be a little brain damaged. I mean, my half-sister Rozy could give a paw when she was three months old. I couldn't.

One day at the beach, I cleared a fence, or rather I didn't and bashed both back paws. No sweat, I was just fine. Until later that night when my paws swelled to twice their normal size and I couldn't walk on them. Mum took the next day off work and we went to the vet.

When the vet tried to feel my paws, I tried to bite Mum, not hard, just to tell her I wanted the vet to stop. Eventually, he put a soft muzzle on me and Mum said if he hurt me, she'd bite him herself. I had no doubt that she would too! Luckily, no broken bones but I got some doggy painkillers because my paws were really sore.

Now, I've been able to swim since I was about five months old when I waded into the sea and started, well... swimming. The sea forms pools on the beach as it's ebbing and these can be unexpectedly deep. The first time I walked into one of these, Dad walked beside me to make sure I didn't freak out and he ended up waist high in water, giving Mum the thumbs up as she watched nervously from dry land. Numpties.

You'd think clearing fences at the beach would be a no-no by now. But no... the next time I tried it, I cleared it beautifully but there was 6ft of sea water on the other side. AAAArrrrggggghh. I like to gradually walk in and find the depth I'm comfy at and this was **way** out of my comfort zone. Dad squealed laughing, but it wasn't so funny when he saw how freaked out I was, scrabbling at the fence with my paws, eyes wild and pure panic oozing from every orifice. He had to fish me out, got soaked again and once more had to walk home like the creature from the black lagoon. Who's laughing now eh, laughing boy?

The woods around our house are lovely and we go there a lot. It didn't take long for my folks to realise they had to make

sure they threw my ball away from trees and steep cliffs because I'd just focus right in and chase the ball. One day, doing just that, I ran full tilt into a park bench. **Ouch!**

Back to the vets, but luckily, no shattered eye socket, just a very nasty split above my eye, no stitches required but the fur will never grow back and I have a very manly scar. Dad thinks it makes me look well hard, Mum is devastated.

As well as all that, they've stood on me and caught my tiny little paws in doors, all by accident.

I'm very lucky to be alive.

When I was seven months old, apparently, I developed a very unhealthy relationship with my toy Tigger and watching from the wings, six year old Shane was asking questions Granny Midge just wasn't prepared to answer.

Off to the vet again. This time, Mum was talking in hushed tones with the nurse about castration, after care, blood tests. She told the nurse I'd had nothing to eat or drink since the night before and she gave me a big hug and loads of kisses. She started to cry and the nurse hugged her tight, then led me away. When I realised Mum wasn't coming with us, I tried to go after her and barked like crazy to get her attention. What was she thinking?

They say that Mum cried so much her head looked like a pumpkin but when she left, they gave me an injection and off I went to snoozypoos.

The next thing I remember is waking up in a strange place in a cage. A CAGE! I hadn't slept in one of those since I was five months old. So I barked and barked for someone to let me out, but no-one did. Thank goodness, I eventually heard Mum's voice, and Nana's and Grandad's but I couldn't see them, so I barked and barked some more. I knew they had come to rescue me, they just needed to know where I was.

The nurse put this strange plastic lamp shade around my neck and took me to Mum. They talked about how to help me recover as quickly as possible. Recover from what? I was fine – well I would be when I got rid of this stupid lampshade. I struggled with the lamp shade and they took it off but told Mum to make sure I didn't lick my scar. She was crying again (does the woman ever stop?) and hugging me – but really gently. When we got to the car, she lifted me in and sat beside me cuddling me, Grandad drove us home and Nana kept looking back from the front seat to check on me. They all spoke very quietly and gently and talked to me in the baby voice again – and I wondered what on earth was going on.

It was hardly a scar really, they'd removed my little boy bumps then glued me back together again. Yes glue....blue it was too. Tasted yummy.

The vet said I could have some water and a little food as soon as I got home. I could have gentle exercise on the lead for a week, gradually building up to my normal walks.

Mum took the week off work to look after me and we both slept downstairs that first night after my operation. She didn't want me rampaging up and down the stairs and damaging myself.

I was desperate to lick my scar, she was desperate that I didn't. I went into corners and hid from her, she followed me. I

wouldn't wear the lampshade so she put one of her old vests on me and pinned it at the bottom like a romper suit so I couldn't get in for a good lick. It was a long night but eventually we slept.

I was pretty much as right as rain the next day and completely back to being the old "me" in just a couple of days. We kept the walks fairly gentle for two to three days and as luck would have it, the weather was fairly decent so I didn't get covered in mud or anything icky and do you know what, these days you can't even see the scar. Mum is so impressed that she's going to ask the vet to do her tummy tuck when she's saved up enough money.

I'm used to a calm home, no-one so much as raises a voice in our house. My folks don't really go out that much. They use weekends to catch up with each other and sometimes they'll invite friends around to catch up with them too. Our philosophy is:

"Fizz lives here, if you don't like that, don't visit"

but most people love me, so it's no problem.

We had a few friends round one night and Mum was saying how Rozy could give a paw and I couldn't. It was bugging her because of course, I was the most intelligent dog – **ever.**

So for hours that night, Uncle David sat with me and played catch with my favourite piece of rag. Rag had started life as a soft ball on a length of stretchy material and I loved it so much that I'd chewed it almost into oblivion and only a scrap of material remained. Apart from Tigger, it was and still is, my favourite possession. Every time he threw the rag, I'd bring it

back to him; he'd gently tap the back of my front paw and throw it again. Eventually, as he tapped my leg and said "paw" at the same time, I'd lift my front leg. By the end of that night, I knew what they wanted when they said "paw" and they were ecstatic. The rag, by that time, was dripping in Fizz spit. Uncle David threw it one last time and it landed down the back of Aunty Jenny's beautiful cocktail dress.

She screamed.

Uncle David didn't even try to hide the huge grin on his face…his aim was getting distinctly better.

Another "quiet night in" and Uncle Barry, Aunty Jules and Uncle Ken came round for a nice meal (don't worry, Dad cooked) I just sat on my cushion in the lounge, minding my own business, chewing my chew, when all hell broke loose…

After a couple of bottles of wine, they put an ABBA CD on. Now that's ok, I like ABBA. Then they started singing along to the tunes. Still ok.

Then they started singing **and dancing.** OMG my Dad was…**dancing…** Please God make it stop. No-one really knows how I did it, but I fled the house.

By the time everyone left and the parents were locking up, they realised with absolute horror that I was nowhere to be found. They searched the garden, went out looking up the street, over the fields and back again. By this time, at 4am, totally panic stricken that I was out somewhere in the dark all alone, total despair set in.

Then the phone rang.

"Fizz is here" said Nana Tosh. "And he's staying here. Don't think of coming for him until morning."

I'd somehow sneaked out of the house, crossed a busy main road and barked at Nana's front door 'til she heard me and let me in. It took a while, Nana is deaf as a post. She says she'll get a restraining order to protect me if they ever do that again.

I've only run away a couple more times since then. It didn't have anything to do with the trauma of my parents singing and dancing, I mean, they stopped that nonsense the first time I went missing, but happened when we were walking in the dark winter nights. My hearing is really acute and something freaked me out in the dark and I headed for home without waiting for them. Now, they put me on a lead when we walk in the dark - an extendable one so I can still run about.

Oh very funny, you'll have to let me out of this garden for exercise soon...

CHAPTER 18

Graduation Day Disaster

"If your dog doesn't like someone, maybe you shouldn't either"

June at puppy school, recognised fairly early on that I wasn't really motivated by food. Sure, I like yummy treats but if I have the choice between a ball and a juicy bit of chicken, I'll usually go for the ball.

By pure instinct, I've adopted the "Collie Crouch" I place the ball or toy where I want it, crouch down and stare at it intently until someone picks it up and throws it. I believe it's very important to keep your humans mind's alert so I sometimes hide the ball down a rabbit hole, place it strategically on a stone, or my personal favourite, on top of some poo so they pick that up as well as the ball. Mum carries wet wipes with her for that very purpose.

When I drop my ball in rabbit holes they say **"Wait"** to stop me going after it in case the rabbit in residence tries to rip my face off.

All of my toys are in a toy box. I know I can chew anything at all in the box, sometimes I even chew the box, but I get the **"No Fizz"** business if I try to chew anything else. I love ripping the stuffing out of soft toys and throwing it all over the house. I've decided that I can chew anything in the garden too, so none of our garden ornaments have ears, fingers or feet and Granny's garden lights are in bits. I have adopted my own style of topiary so our bushes and trees are unusual to say the least and I've dug Nana's new conifers out a gazillion times. It hasn't stopped me taking huge chunks out of Granny's skirting boards and wardrobes... and Dad's walking boots but generally I stick to the rules.

Whilst I was usually very good at puppy school, recall was a problem. We practiced on the beach and in the woods but if something interesting was going on elsewhere, off I went to investigate. No amount of tempting treats or calling after me would persuade me to come back until I was good and ready. I want to please them, I do. But the urge to please myself is always stronger.

They tried hide and seek, where I would run off and they would hide somewhere where they could see me but I couldn't see them. I must admit, the first time they tried that, I panicked and stayed very close for the rest of that walk. But actually, I'm an excellent sniffer so the opportunities to hide without being sniffed out were limited.

June suggested that rather than treats, they always take a squeaky toy out on our walks and when I'm tempted to run away, they squeak or throw the toy. Works every time for me. When I have a toy, I'm not remotely interested in people or dogs and they can direct me away from oncoming cyclists or joggers just by throwing something in a different direction or wagging a rope at me to pull on.

Now and again, I'll lose my toys. There's a string of plastic sausages lodged high up in the branches of a tree, dozens of balls down rabbit holes and a squeaky pork chop somewhere in the woods. We usually take a "spare" in case we lose something but if we lose that as well, I pick up a stick. For a while, I only wanted sticks and gradually these got bigger and bigger until I was cavorting around with huge logs. This had to stop after I took them both out at the knees with an especially large log. I was weaned off sticks very quickly and reverted back to toys. ***Top tip:*** *"Pound shops" and second hand shops are great for cheap toys, don't buy expensive stuff if it's likely that it'll be lost, we really don't know the difference. Don't buy small stuff that we can choke on and for great exercise, balls on ropes can be lobbed huge distances. Don't ever throw sticks for your dog, they're very dangerous and cause horrific injuries.*

There was great excitement on puppy school graduation day. We were having a puppy party with tons of treats and games. We always did our homework and we'd been following our checklist, so I'd been introduced to all the visitors to our home – the bin men, window cleaner, neighbours and friends. I'd been walked past schools with lots of screechy children. I'd been introduced to lots of other dogs, cats, hamsters and Bruce the guinea pig who lives next door. We had practiced sit, stand, down, stay, heel and recall and were pretty confident I would do well on graduation day.

Oh dear.

Ben and Nemmy managed recall in under 2 seconds and won biscuits. As Dad was frantically beckoning and calling for me, I sat there looking at him, wagging my tail then I wandered over to Ben for a sniff. I never completed the exercise and was disqualified.

I started really well at slalom, weaving in and out of skittles, following a nice bit of mackerel Dad had in his fingers. Then Skye barked and I turned to look at her, flicking the last skittle with my tail. That earned me penalty points but the worst bit was Nana getting to her feet and needing to be restrained amid claims that I'd been "knobbled."

I was useless at "heel" because I had to walk past all the other puppies and I just wanted to play. I was quite good at the examination bit where Ben's Dad checked my ears, between my toes and felt my bones but still rolled over for a tickle and think I may have lost points when he lifted my tail and I bit him. Well, it was a bit familiar don't you think?

The final humiliation came when Mum and Dad had to bandage my paw. A useful skill when you romp around in long grass and some idiot has thrown glass or tin in there. I wriggled and squirmed and had great fun ripping the bandage to shreds and when June blew the whistle for us to stop, all the other puppies had a bandaged paw of some description and I had bits of bandage and string all over the floor. My Dad is the "first aider" for his company. May God help them all, they'll bleed to death before he gets his head around how to get a bandage to stay on.

It's fair to say that I didn't graduate with honours, Moll gave me biscuits out of sympathy because I was the only pup that didn't actually win any. We didn't stay around afterwards to celebrate, socialise or agree to meet up again to practice what we'd learned. We just slid into the car and headed for the sanctuary of home.

The learning process continues and as well as plentiful walks, practicing the basics like sit, paw and so on, we have playtime. This means different things to different people. Mum hides treats and I have to work out how to get them, Dad wrestles with me, me and Grandad play footie, I'm a pretty nifty goalie. Nana is teaching me all the names of my toys and I can fetch ball, pig, dragon, dumbbell and snoopy when she asks me to, Granny chases me like a mad woman around the house. I think it's important to keep them active, otherwise they become bored and disruptive.

Romping on "our" beach

CHAPTER 19

Wantonly abandoned and christening our new kitchen

"If your dog is fat, you aren't getting enough exercise"

Being left on your own is a bit scary to say the least.

At first, I was only left on my own at night time and I would go into my snuggly cage. I liked it best when they covered it up with a sheet because it was nice and dark and cosy and I'd just drift off to sleep.

For some reason, they decided that they would have to try and leave me alone fairly early on. So on day three, they kissed me, put me in my cage with a toy stuffed with treats *Top Tip: put pate or cream cheese in the top of these toys then put them in the freezer, that keeps the treats inside for longer and it tastes yummy.* They made sure there was water in my coop cup, covered the cage with my sheet and left the house.

What were they thinking? My cage door was always left open when it was light outside. I'd just go in and out as I pleased. Sometimes I'd wander in for some peace to get away from the mad people but I was never locked in in **daylight**. There must be some horrible mistake, so I was yipping and yapping before they'd left the room. "Mum, Dad, come back, you've forgotten me, we go everywhere together....do, do, don't we?"

Nothing.

How was I to know if they were ever coming back?

Unbeknown to me, they were standing at the front door with the letter box open listening to make sure I'd settle. Dad was trying to be a man about it but Mum was stressed to death. Sure enough in less than five minutes, I quietened down and turned my attention to licking my toy and I set about releasing whatever they had hidden inside.

They were gone for less than half an hour and came straight into the kitchen to get me. In spite of this atrocious act of neglect, I was ridiculously pleased to see them and wriggled around in a heightened state of excitement "Oh you're back, you're back, let me jump on you and bite you, what's in the bag? Something for me, let me look, tickle my tummy."

I'm never left for long stretches at a time. Maybe a couple of hours, now and then. Granny's at home 'til lunchtime, Dad comes home in his lunch break and we have a walk. Uncle Neil and Aunty Nicola come for me if they're not at work and my cousins Danielle and Keri come for me when they can. At home, me and Mum have FizziFridays and I go to Nana's if she has to work or go somewhere. On the rare occasions Mum and Dad go somewhere they can't take me, I go to Nana's. Sometimes I stay overnight.

I've never stayed in kennels. Whilst there are some extremely good ones, my Mum couldn't bear the thought of me being away from all of my family, so when they go on holiday I stay with Granny or Nana. That's just fine because I'm used to being with them anyway.

The first time they went on holiday I was only three months old. It was their wedding anniversary and they went to a lovely country spa for the weekend. I stayed with my Nana Tosh. There was no need to pack my bed, food, toys, treats, poo bags or anything really because I have everything I need at home, at Nana's and at Granny's. Nana and Granny have both been to puppy school so they know how to behave properly around me.

In September, it was a little more serious, they were going to Egypt to visit Aunty Dawn and Uncle Mamo for **two whole weeks.**

Granny took a week off work and on the day they left, we all got up at about five in the morning, went into the garden and Mum kept cuddling me. She gave me a big slobbery tearful kiss, Dad said "Stoppit, you're upsetting him" then took me upstairs, gave me a big slobbery tearful kiss and I went to sleep on Granny's bed.

Grandad came to collect me the second week and me, Grandad and Nana spent a week on the beach. Sometimes Aunty Sandra and my cousin Lauren would come and take me out too. I know I'm very lucky to have such a devoted family and it was great, I didn't miss the parents at all. Even though they rang every day to see how I was doing.

When they came home and walked into Nana's garden where I was lying sunning myself, I went **loopy!** Maybe I hadn't missed them but I was nearly as ecstatic as they were to be reunited.

The cream kitchen floor was really getting to Mum. The tiles were rough stone and even before I arrived, it was sheer hard work keeping them clean. After I arrived, it was damned near

98

impossible. One day, when we went to the fields beside our house for a walk, I trotted into a little pond. Except it wasn't really a pond, I'd managed to sheep-dip myself in green slime and was covered up to my neck. Interesting aroma…

It was a wide berth all the way home and a number of gentle sprays with the garden hose for me when we got back. Try as they might, I was green and stinking to high heaven for a couple of days and had somehow ingrained the slime into the kitchen tiles.

They just had to go.

But that meant a whole new kitchen …didn't it? Well not really, but when her mind is made up there isn't any point in arguing. So Mum dragged Dad around all the kitchen showrooms and they settled on a hi-tech, cream and black, high gloss with black granite sci-fi kitchen.

The walls are now covered in cream washable paint so when I go swishing past with a muddy tail, it's easy to wipe clean, and finally…

The last thing to be fitted was the stressed black ash, driftwood floor. Beautiful.

The dreaded cream floor was gone. Replaced with a lovely, easy to clean, black floor. It still shows all my muddy paw prints so it gets a mop around every day but instead of taking hours, it now takes minutes.

The black high gloss units were not such a bright idea, unless of course you think they are vastly improved when adorned with wet nose marks…oh well, you can't have it all.

 99

The sticks started to get bigger and bigger

CHAPTER 20

Becoming a man and trying to understand their weird rituals

"Don't accept your dog's adoration as conclusive evidence that you are wonderful"

October to December proved quite eventful. It started when, for no apparent reason, gangs of strange creatures knocked on our door incessantly. The constant knocking was bad enough, but when we opened the door, there stood witches, devils, ghouls and actually, a rather fetching werewolf. Mum gave them sweeties to make them go away. No matter how much I barked at them, it didn't stop them banging on our door and scaring me witless every time the door opened. Fortunately, it stopped as suddenly as it had started. Not so for my next ordeal...

For a few days I could hear gun shots in the distance. It got more and more frequent and seemed to be creeping closer to our house. I'd slink around the house looking for somewhere to hide. When one horrible bang went off, I climbed into my Mum's shoe cupboard. No amount of coaxing, even with yummy treats, would get me to come out. Next time we heard a loud bang, we were in the car and I had to be carried out, wriggling and resisting as best I could. I wouldn't eat my tea and decided not to go out at all in the dark – around 5 pm. Mum's anxieties about me peeing and pooing started all over again as I'd go from mid-afternoon to 8 o'clock the next morning. She decided to put a lead on me and take me out in the dark. Stupid woman.

First of all, I hate being on a lead, secondly, once outside, the bangs came along with horrible fizzy noises and flashes of light. It was only a short walk up the street but I crawled under every car, behind every bush and in the corner of every doorway. It was horrible and I didn't do a single pee or poo.

They got my cage out of the garage and put it on the landing; they filled it with a big cushion, toys and treats. The idea was to give me somewhere safe and cosy to hide when the noises got too much. Didn't work, not even when Tigger made an appearance on the cushion.

Off we went to the vet again. In yet another act of wanton neglect, Mum had left it too late to get me some gentle calming treatments like a diffuser, a collar or a CD with noises on to de-sensitise me over time before Bonfire Night.

That stuff takes time to take effect; so the vet checked my heart and prescribed diazepam. DIAZEPAM! The parents were shocked and upset. They decided that I would only get it if I was really upset so I lay on the sofa with Nana for a couple of nights. Having a deaf Nana is quite handy; the television in her house is always pretty loud and I got tons of cuddles. The next night – actual Bonfire Night – Dad lay on the bed with me, we watched the telly and every time there was a loud noise we'd comfort each other. So no diazepam and we'll all be better prepared next time this stupidity kicks off.

Our vet recommends that you should just go about your normal business when the loud bangs go off. Let your dog

know this is normal and act naturally. Don't make any fuss or your dog will associate it with something scary.

We saw a lady on the beach blowing up balloons and letting her dogs chase and burst them. Mum asked what she was doing "I'm getting them used to loud bangs ahead of Bonfire Night. They associate the noise with play and it stops them being so scared." Seems logical but I really don't fancy it myself!

On 26th November I did my first "cocky leg man pee" and as luck would have it, both parents were there to witness this momentous occasion. Mum sent texts to all her family and friends to say that I was finally a man because I peed like one (!) and most of them texted back with warm congratulations. Mind you, one or two texted back telling her to get a grip…

Thing is, it's a bit like pooing outside my garden, I did it that once and have never done it since.

On 7th December, we celebrated my birthday. I had a lovely pupcake with one candle. I gave Mum a high five, she blew out the candle and I ate my cake. There wasn't much point in offering it around because, even though Mum hadn't baked it herself, they didn't seem to fancy it. Liver cake – what's not to love?

Turning a year old was a bit of a landmark for me. My puppy book said that my senses would be developing all the time and from 6 months to 18 months, things might freak me out that hadn't before. That was certainly true. For absolutely no good reason, I developed a totally irrational fear of plastic bags. Well not of the bags, but of the rustling noise they make.

When anyone rustles a plastic bag, I run for cover.

Have you ever tried to make your world plastic bag free? It's damned near impossible. My dental sticks come in plastic bags, our weekly shop arrives in plastic bags and my poo bags are plastic; aaaaarrrrgggghh is there no escape from my torment?

Mum has replaced her shopping bags with fabric ones (see… my aversion is saving the planet) but Aunty Fee said to put my favourite toy in a placky bag and rustle it so I would see that good things happen when I hear that noise. Not working…yet.

I've also become ever so slightly anti-social. The "He's not allowed upstairs" rule only lasted a couple of months until I started sleeping on Mum and Dad's bed with them. Then I discovered there was a whole double bed that no-one slept on, so I now sleep there. When it gets noisy downstairs, or someone rustles plastic, or when I just want to be alone, I head on up to the spare room (now known as Fizz's Room) and have a kip. Mum and Dad keep coming up and checking on me. This bothered them until Aunty Fee said "He's obviously secure and stress free. If he was unhappy, he'd be under your feet". I always wander into Mum and Dad's room at about 7am for wrestling with Dad and cuddles with Mum.

Two weeks after my birthday Dad went into the loft. I barked at the ladders and tried to get him to come down. He was handing boxes to Mum, so I barked at them too.

Then for absolutely no good reason, this great big tree was assembled in our living room, it was covered in all manner of tasteless gaudiness and I hated it. To add insult to injury, a

three foot reindeer with a bloody red nose appeared and stood in our hallway and a choir of stuffed characters sang "We wish you a Merry Christmas" every time we walked past them.

Not content with all of that, a big, silver, tinselly, cone thing with a light inside went into the kitchen...I barked incessantly at the lot of them, what abject madness was going on now?

Thank goodness, Nana and Grandad came to stay a couple of days later and I slept peacefully on my bed with them ...until we woke up, and even more madness ensued.

There were parcels and boxes all over our living room. Everyone started ripping paper and the phone was ringing incessantly, so I crawled up beside Nana for refuge. I knew something was going on because me and Dad are not allowed on the living room furniture, yet Nana cuddled me in and let me stay.

Apparently a significant number of the parcels were for me and my already full toy box was now overflowing with plastic doggy newspapers, squeakies, balls, all manner of treats and rope toys.

This Santa bloke they kept telling me about was certainly generous.

A couple of weeks ago I got a card in the post. It was addressed to me and said "Hi Fizz, it's a year since your vaccination. It's time for your booster and health check, Love St Francis Veterinary Care."

So off we went, back to the vet. I had my booster, had ears, bones, muscles, heart, chest, toes and eyes checked. I got scanned to make sure my chip was still in place.

They discussed diet, exercise, behaviour and the vet said I was a fit and content one year old and I can now move gradually to adult dog food – oh boy! I've been enjoying my lovely grub for months now and yes, they still chop chicken, liver, ham etc., into it to stop it becoming boring. I have two different flavours that they alternate but it looks like the hunt for adult food is on ...Help me...

This apparently, is my stocking. Not only does it not fit, there's only one!

CHAPTER 21

….and finally,

"Properly trained, a man can be dog's best friend"

So here we are, a year on. It hasn't always been easy, there have been tears but also lots of laughs. We've got gazillions of happy memories, like me trying to catch the rain, the first time I ever saw snow, Mum sliding uncontrollably, down a hill in the mud, me running off with the stick Granny was using to steady herself with, trying to get to my Mum in a mirror and banging my head, chasing mops and brushes and my legendary, flatulence. Oh yes, I was getting away with that one until I was neutered. Apparently I broke wind more loudly and frequently than any other dog in history on that operating table and the nurse dobbed me in to Mum. It's a real shame as it caused another food frenzy to change to something more socially acceptable and worse still, Mum doesn't blame Dad for the horrendous smell anymore.

I'm every bit a fully paid up member of this family and my needs are considered along with everyone else's when any decisions are made. I'm very lucky because there always seems to be someone to keep me company most of the time.

My family had no idea that having a dog is such a huge responsibility, I'm totally dependent on them for love and care, decent food and fresh water and, at least two decent walks every single day in all weathers. Holidays can't be booked until I'm safely taken care of and then they pine for

me when we're apart. We're all very excited to be going on holiday together this year. Dog's Trust have holiday cottages on their website where dogs go free. There are also a number of hotels where dogs can stay. Be careful to check out charges and where the hotels expect your dog to stay, some insist they can't stay in the rooms and have kennel accommodation somewhere on the premises – that's not for us, we like to share facilities.

I go to the vet every month for my flea treatment and every three months I get a worm tablet. When I'm there, I get weighed. You might be tempted to buy treatments on the internet or in the supermarket, just make sure they are reputable companies or you risk harming your precious pet. Also make sure you give them the right amount for their weight. Under or overdosing is dangerous, it might be best to wait until your puppy's weight stabilises at around 12 – 18 months. **Never, ever** give a dog medicine intended for humans. Some human medicine is fatal for dogs and anyway, you would have no idea what dosage to give them.

One of the cruellest things you can do is overfeed a dog. I never get chocolate or human sweeties, which are really bad for dogs. I get delicious complete, dry dog food which gives me everything I need and keeps my eyes bright and my coat glossy. For treats, I get cooked chicken, ham, or liver. You don't have to spend a fortune on treats, dog treats are available in all supermarkets but a slab of cooked liver or "own brand" sausages or pate, cost pennies and are much yummier. Because I get lots of exercise – about 2 hours a day, and I play a lot with my toys, I get treats every day in moderation.

If someone is at our door, or if I hear a strange noise, I bark and they let me. They say in a calm voice "What is it Fizz, go

see…?" I mean, if there was a burglar around, they'd want me to scare him off. If I bark outside, Mum or Dad will come out to investigate and distract me with a toy so that I don't annoy our neighbours. Rabbits live with the people next door to us and one of them hopped into our garden (the rabbit, that is. I don't think the people are very accomplished "hoppers".) I was ecstatic and ran over to play but he went through a tiny hole in our fence and Dad went and blocked the hole up. Killjoy, we could have been mates.

As well as lovely walks in lots of different places to keep me interested, we play lots of games. This might be footie in the garden, fetching a particular toy, retrieving some delicious yumminess from a toy you can fill with treats, playing tuggy with a ropey, even dancing with Nana. Sometimes, they hide treats around the house and garden and I sniff them out. I dug a pile of bulbs up from our flower beds and chewed them, they were rubbish treats so I spat them on the lawn. I've dug up countless bushes and plants and our lawn has never recovered from last year when I turned it into a swamp. Be careful what you plant in your garden, some stuff is poisonous for pets – read the labels.

The house is still pretty much cream leather and voile (apart from our black kitchen) but now it has tail brush marks across the doors and splash marks up the walls. Mum constantly walks around with a damp cloth in her hand.

I'm totally house trained now, but still have the odd little accident. In fact, I peed in the hall just the other day. No idea why, it's the first time in months and months, so when it was spotted Mum said to me "What's this?" and I wriggled and squirmed and licked my Mum to say sorry. She told me I was naughty in a very calm voice and I stayed scarce for a few

minutes and all was forgiven. I hardly ever get the "naughty" word but I know I've done something bad when they say it.

I rarely try to bite the parents when they brush me now. I quite like it actually. They brush me when I'm sleepy and it relaxes me. Thing is, they have to wait until I roll over before they can brush the other side because rolling me over when I'm snoozy is a biteable offence!

I don't really need to have a bath because I get brushed and I go to the beach or the riverside where I usually have a little swim. I sometimes have to stay in the garden and get cleaned up with a bucket and sponge before I'm allowed in the house and I quite like a gentle hose down. Be sure not to have the hose too strong, that's not very nice at all. I've also never had my nails clipped yet. The vet checks them every month but I get a "pedicure" by running on the beach at least a couple of times a week.

We live in a very calm household. No-one shouts – well, unless Newcastle score a goal on the telly, and Dad turns into a loony. We all get along just fine. Having a dog changes your life but, we can't bear to be apart for long now. I sometimes go into my bedroom for some quiet time but we never close the doors inside our house. We can all roam around as we please and it's never long before one of them pops a head around the door and comes in for a cuddle.

I'm not really a "morning dog" I get up early during the week for a walk with Dad before he goes to work, but then I go back to bed and cuddle up with Granny, making sure I put muddy paws everywhere except the dust sheet she puts on her bed for me. I'm happy having a lie in at the weekends because I know we'll probably go somewhere new and interesting for a

walk. Sometimes, we'll pack a bag and just head off somewhere nice. I have my own picnic stuff – water bottle, treat box and a toy to throw around. We stop somewhere pretty like a river or lake for lunch and walk back. It might take up most of the day but we all love it.

I've pretty much broken every rule they ever made, for example: Fizz won't be allowed:

- upstairs – lasted about three months,
- at the table when we're eating – my bean bag is in the kitchen and my cushion is in the dining room, I am not made of stone!
- to greed from people – well, is it my fault if they tear a little bit off their sandwich and give it to me?
- to pull on the lead – I can't help it, I need to get there before you do…
- to jump up at people – I get so excited but I do get "down" when I'm told.

and make a liar out of them every time they say something silly like, "You can leave your plate there, he won't touch it" – **come on people!**

Top tip: If you don't know if you can manage a dog of your own, try having a friend's dog for the holidays or volunteer at a local shelter. If you can't spare an hour or so a day to walk, feed and play with a homeless dog how on earth are you ever going to manage a dog of your own? And you never know, you may find the dog of your dreams.

Puppies need endless patience, they won't understand what you are trying to tell them for **months and months.** Don't be tempted to lose your temper, it doesn't make them

understand any better, it just makes them frightened. Just keep calmly trying to train them to behave nicely. Give treats, cuddles, tickles and praise **all the time.**

Discipline should be uncomplicated – one word such as "naughty" or "bad" in a stern voice will get your message over – eventually.

Well, that's our tail (sorry!) such as it is. I hope you've enjoyed being with us and maybe we'll meet again sometime.

None of us are perfect but I love them and they love me. On that note, I leave the last quote to my Dad:

"Half the world loves my dog. The other half are just missing out"

Acknowledgements

Sincere thanks to Aunty Fee, aka Fiona Middleton; Pete and Barbara; June, Moll and Eileen at Pawfect; Practice Manager Julie, nurses, receptionists and vets at St Clair Veterinary Care and all my family for helping to take care of me. Special thanks to my Aunty Christine Adamson for love, support and proof reading.

Quotes taken from, The Perfect Puppy by Gwen Bailey; The Little Book of Humorous Quotations; A Dog's Life, an inspiration for dog lovers everywhere; Everything Dogs Expect You to Know, Karen Bush; Quotable Animals, Milly Brown; Original Wit, Des MacHale, Wise Cracks, everyday wit and wisdom, Tom Burns. Plus some that my Mum and Dad made up themselves.

We got the following letter sent to us by email, so we have no idea who the original author is but whoever you are, thanks, it made us laugh and we hope you don't mind us sharing it:

Dear Dogs and Cats,
The dishes with the paw prints on are yours and contain your food. The other dishes are mine and contain my food. Placing a paw print in the middle of my plate does not make it your food and dish, nor do I find that aesthetically pleasing.

The stairway was not designed by NASCAR and is not a racetrack. Racing me to the bottom is not the object. Tripping me doesn't help because I fall faster than you run.

I cannot buy anything bigger than a king sized bed. I am very sorry about this, however dogs and cats can actually curl up in a ball to sleep. It is not necessary to stretch out to the fullest extent possible. I also know that sticking tails straight out and hanging tongues out at the other end to maximise space is nothing but sarcasm.

For the last time, there is no secret exit from the bathroom. If by some miracle, I beat you there and manage to get the door shut, it is not necessary to claw, whine, meow, try to turn the door handle or get your paw under the door in an attempt to get in. I must exit from the same door I entered. Believe me, I have been using the bathroom for years. Canine/feline attendance is not necessary.

The proper order for kissing is: kiss me first then sniff another dog/cat's butt. I cannot stress this enough.

When they calm down, I'll let them out

And to all non-pet owners who visit my house:

- *they live here, you don't;*
- *if you don't want hair on your clothes, stay off my furniture;*
- *I prefer my pets to most people;*
- *to you they are animals, to me they are adopted sons/daughters who are short, hairy, walk on all fours and don't speak clearly;*
- *if you don't want me to comment on your kids' behaviour, don't criticise my pets.*